T0287641

Cricket, My Brother and Me!

Geoff Hart

Cricket, My Brother and Me!

Fifty Years Watching English Cricket

First published by Pitch Publishing, 2022

Pitch Publishing
9 Donnington Park,
85 Birdham Road,
Chichester,
West Sussex,
PO20 7AJ
www.pitchpublishing.co.uk
info@pitchpublishing.co.uk

ISBN 978 1 80150 116 3

Typesetting and origination by Pitch Publishing
Printed and bound in Great Britain by TJ Books Ltd

Contents

For my Dad, Gerald John Hart

1917-1991

(known to everyone as 'Gerry')

He left my brother and me a precious
gift: the love of cricket.

This book is based on my
recollection of events and
conversations from my
memories of them.

Acknowledgements

I WOULD like to thank my fellow members of Llandudno & District Writers Club, particularly those who form the Critique Group. They have read virtually every chapter of this book making valuable comments and coming up with excellent suggestions. I especially wish to thank those members of the group who displayed such stoicism in reading and critiquing the text despite their complete lack of affinity to cricket.

My thanks also to my wife, Marieluise, and my daughter, Lucy, for proofreading the text with eagle eyes.

To my two daughters, Emily and Lucy, as well as their husbands, Andrew and Tom and my friend Ewen: thank you for sharing my cricket journey.

Thanks to my grandchildren, Finlay and Iris, who seem more than willing to carry the flame.

Finally, above all, I would like to thank Roy, with whom I have shared a love of cricket through our entire lifetime. I could not have wished for a better brother.

Photographic Acknowledgements

The author would like to thank the following for permission to reproduce photographs:

Regatta Bar: courtesy of Marzena Photography
Trent Bridge: courtesy of Nottinghamshire CCC
Paddy Powell: courtesy of Tony (Reckless) Hammond
Getty Images
Alamy
All other photographs are from my private collection

Chapter One

Down and Out, Down Under

I COULD see the ferry approaching and instinctively started to run. I arrived at the Regatta just as the ferry docked, but turning round saw Roy still more than a hundred yards behind me. We had travelled halfway round the world to watch a game of cricket and thanks to my brother's notorious swollen ankles we were going to miss the start. The ferryman read the anxiety in my face.

'Don't worry, mate. There's another one along in ten minutes. At that speed he should arrive just right.'

And with that he pulled up the gangplank that doubled as a gate and continued along the Brisbane River in the direction of the holy Gabba, the Brisbane Cricket Ground that derives its odd nickname from the suburb of Woolloongabba, in which it is located.

Roy's ankles, always slightly pudgy, had swollen to the size of pomegranates during the long flight and he had been seeking sympathy ever since. However, what I was feeling at that moment was naked hostility. I gave him a hard stare, not all that effective from a distance of a hundred yards, but it made me feel better. Unexpectedly he reacted by breaking into a gentle trot. He therefore arrived at the boarding point in good time for the next ferry which, as promised, appeared ten minutes later. Gratefully we stepped aboard.

The ferry route from the Regatta terminal near our apartment in Auchenflower passed under the Go-Between Bridge before following a right-hand bend in the river and heading towards the Victoria Bridge. Along this stretch the whole city opens up before you. Brisbane is an unlikely but very successful blend of attractive modern architecture and Victorian grandeur, the latter reflecting its colonial history. Beyond the Victoria Bridge the ferry makes a brief stop at the beautiful South Bank Parklands with its public lawns, gardens, swimming areas and awesome man-made beaches. It is also the site of the enormous Wheel of Brisbane, built in 2008 to celebrate the 150th anniversary of the State of Queensland.

The ferry continues on under the Goodwill Bridge before docking at the Maritime Museum, a short walk from the Gabba.

It soon became clear that almost everyone on board was heading to the same event as us. Given the group of passengers included the *Test Match Special* commentator and *Times* journalist, Christopher Martin-Jenkins and Simon Barnes, chief sportwriter of *The Times*, it was fair to assume we would arrive on time after all.

I had never been a big fan of Martin-Jenkins on *TMS*. I much preferred the wayward style of his co-commentator, Henry Blofeld. Roy on the other hand liked CMJ as he was known, particularly favouring his extremely precise and well-informed account of every ball. Being an affable sort, it was inevitable that Roy would attempt to strike up a conversation with the man about the prospects for the day's play. Unfortunately, he never got the chance as about 50 other fans had the same idea.

Not for the first time I thought how wonderful it would be to draw a good salary for travelling the globe watching cricket in perpetual summer. If I were in that position you would never be able to wipe the smile off my face. As might be expected there were plenty of other people keen to discuss the cricket, the Australian supporters in particular. As a result, by the time we got off the ferry for the short walk to the ground, I at least was well and truly ready for our adventure to begin. Roy was by contrast still struggling to unwind. He is a massive cricket fan and a real lover of the way the Australians approach the game. I think he was feeling quite overwhelmed by the whole occasion, and I could see it would not take much to tip him over the edge. Soon I would realise how accurate this assessment was.

I have become used to the fact that Roy tends to arrive at cricket matches with a large bag containing every item that he might potentially require. This includes clothing suitable for both the Sahara Desert and an ascent of Everest as well as every weather condition in between. What we did not know was that there was a bag restriction imposed at the Gabba and any item wider than 40cm had to be surrendered at the entrance gate. Roy became instantly on edge at this point as he seemed to believe that he would never see his rucksack again, although the very helpful steward was at pains to explain that one merely surrendered it like a coat at a cloakroom.

He seemed to be calming down and was just handing the bag over when he suddenly convinced himself that he had put the tickets in one of the bag's many pockets. He abruptly took the bag back and started furiously searching in every pocket, cavity and flap of the bag … and then again! He was close to hysteria when I innocently suggested they could be in his jacket or trouser pocket. He yelled at me that they were in the bag, but I ignored him and while he stood there in a catatonic state, I proceeded to go through his pockets. Moments later I held up the tickets, but rather than feeling relieved he remained rigid and appeared to be in some sort of daze. Eventually he grabbed them from my hand and presented them to the bemused steward.

'Have a nice day, mate,' the steward said, at last able to revert to his normal script and we entered the ground with Roy emotionally exhausted before a ball had been bowled.

As we settled into our seats, high above the action, Roy proceeded to introduce himself and me to the group of guys sitting around us. As would be expected they were with the same touring company as us and at least six of them were good friends and had travelled as a group. Roy soon established that they knew their cricket, which was important as we seemed destined to sit amongst them for the whole match.

As the start of play drew nearer Roy began insuring himself against disappointment.

'I presume you know we haven't won at the Gabba since 1986,' was his first pronouncement.

I was ready for him.

'When we faced them in 2005 we hadn't won the Ashes for 18 years. Things change; eras come to an end. You'll see.'

Roy was reneging slightly here. We had harboured the idea of a tour to Australia for many years. We had decided that this was the time to do it because the 2005 series had instilled in us the belief that we could finally win in Australia, not something we had genuinely believed in for a long time.

We sat with our individual thoughts, me visualising an England win at the Gabba while Roy wondered how he would cope with defeat. I had picked up a copy of *Being Freddie* at the airport which included Andrew Flintoff's account of the 2005 campaign.[1] I had it in my bag and decided it would help me to focus on positive thoughts.

In the absence of Michael Vaughan, who was injured, Flintoff had been made captain, a move I approved of whereas Roy would have preferred Andrew Strauss. History was to prove him right.

Suddenly my mobile went off. I stared at the screen on which my daughter Emily's name had appeared. It was 10.50pm at home. I felt mild panic, but answered, nevertheless.

'Hi Dad! You won't believe it. We just saw you on telly.'

'You didn't. Are you sure it was us?'

'Of course I am. I do know my own father. Roy was staring into space – nothing new there – and you were rummaging in your bag. The Gabba looks incredible.'

Emily and her husband Andy had sort of 'lived through' the 2005 Ashes with us and still felt that tie, even though we were now on the other side of the world. I guess that seeing us there at the game made them feel part of it.

'Don't worry, dad. We'll smash 'em.'

I was glad that she was no longer on the phone when Steve Harmison bowled that first ball of the series so wide that it went directly to Andrew Flintoff at second slip. The guy next to me had not yet donned his glasses and for a moment thought it was a catch. Roy soon put him right and I think from then on he thought we were doomed. He wasn't wrong.

I have to admit that at that moment of catastrophe my normal optimism completely deserted me. I had a sinking feeling that is hard to describe. I have only experienced such desperation once since then, on the night of the election in December 2019 when the exit poll predicted a landslide for Boris Johnson. It is a tribute to the human spirit that Roy and I both recovered to enjoy the match and the whole trip.

So far our recovery from the shock of that election has been less robust.

At the end of day one Australia were already 346/3 with Ricky Ponting 137 not out and looking indomitable. Alongside him Michael Hussey seemed very assured on 63. As we walked back to the ferry that evening it was already hard to see how England could win the match from here. Although the possibility of a draw still existed, psychologically I joined Roy in preparing for defeat.

We had decided to make the cricket fan's ultimate pilgrimage to Australia shortly after the 2005 Ashes in England, widely acknowledged as the greatest Test series in the history of the game. Looking forward from that historic success there seemed reason to believe that England could do well again in 2006/07. We had booked through a tour company flying from Heathrow to Brisbane with a change at Hong Kong. The two flights were comfortable and largely uneventful, particularly for Roy who was asleep for most of the time. Eventually we arrived at Brisbane airport with me knackered and Roy fully refreshed having dealt with potential jet lag in the best way possible.

We walked through the airport chatting in that 'well we made it' pioneer sort of way as if no Brit had ever ventured this far before when suddenly our way was barred by a burly Australian policeman. His springer spaniel was showing a lot of interest in my rucksack which for some reason Roy was carrying.

'Could you empty that bag, mate?' the policeman asked Roy who, although somewhat nonplussed, complied at once. The policeman showed no interest in any of the contents until Roy finally pulled out a rather manky banana which I remembered at that moment had been given to me by my daughter Lucy as I left home aboard the transfer bus to Heathrow.

'You can't go 200 miles on the bus with nothing to eat,' she had told me in a very imperious manner. She was the only seasoned traveller in the family. I had accepted the gift, put it into my rucksack and thought no more about it, until now.

'I am formally notifying you that I believe an offence has been committed in contravention of the Food and Agricultural Import Regulations and Standards. As a result ...'

'Excuse me, officer!' Roy had stopped the man in his tracks. Probably a bad idea, I thought. 'If you are arresting me for possession of a banana, you need to know it is not my banana.'

The policeman gave him a quizzical and slightly hostile stare.

'I beg your pardon.'

'It's not my banana,' Roy repeated.

'The banana was found in your bag.'

'It's not my bag.'

'Did someone ask you to carry the bag into Australia for them?'

Roy hesitated for a second before his innate honesty overcame any misguided sense of family loyalty.

'Well, yes. My brother here needed a pee and asked me to hold his bag while he went looking for a toilet.'

The policeman looked at Roy long and hard. He did not seem to like what he saw. Reluctantly he swivelled to face me, holding the banana aloft.

'Is this yours?' he enquired.

It seemed frivolous at this stage to bring my daughter, Lucy, into the equation although in terms of ownership it was strictly speaking her banana. I decided to keep it simple. 'Yes, sir, it is.'

The police officer hesitated, albeit only briefly. 'I am formally notifying you that an offence has been committed in contravention of the Food and Agricultural Import Regulations and Standards, as a result of which I am verbally warning you that any further contravention could result in a fine or a period of imprisonment.'

There was a pause and I was desperate to ask him if that was it, but common sense prevented me. Eventually, I was informed that the banana was being confiscated and the police officer started to walk away, no doubt glad to see the back of us. The springer spaniel on the other hand looked back at me with a slight snarl as if to say, 'I've got your number, mate.'

We had booked our trip down under with a well-known tour company which did a great job in every respect bar one. We had made the booking relatively late and the huge hotel where everybody else was accommodated was already full. As a result, we were billeted in a self-catering apartment in one of Brisbane's inner suburbs. When we opened the door to the apartment we couldn't believe our eyes. Except for the bathroom, the whole apartment was one gigantic room about 50 feet long. At first we weren't sure what we thought about it, but given the positive mood we were in decided it was some sort of privilege to be allocated so much space! Also, with the beds so far apart it meant that Roy's snoring would not be a problem. The only real downside was its suburban location a good two miles from the centre of town and what we perceived as 'the action'. However, once we discovered that the Brisbane River, complete with regular ferries in each direction, was only spitting distance from our lodgings we were happy enough. It probably meant that we missed out on the official company welcome and tour T-shirt, but that wasn't high on our list of priorities.

On our first day in Brisbane we wandered along the river taking in the sights and stopping for the occasional beer. At one stop for 'refreshments' we sat outside with our drinks and watched a beautiful exotic bird as it hopped around from table to table. We were just eulogising over the bird's unusual markings and vivid colours when the barman came across and flicked a tea towel at it.

'Bloody pigeons!' he exclaimed as the bird flew off, no doubt seeking a more hospitable environment. One man's exotic bird is another man's vermin, it seems.

Later that evening we made a fine discovery. Not more than 40 yards from our apartment was an excellent Chinese restaurant. We spent an enjoyable evening there and made a note to return, which we did several times. During the course of the evening the jet lag started to catch up with me big style so we decided to call it a day. When we arrived at the entrance to the flat we realised that we had left the keys on the restaurant table so Roy went back to fetch them. I sat down on the step and immediately fell into a deep sleep. When he returned Roy had some difficulty rousing me.

'It's just lucky someone else didn't find you first,' he said.

The following morning I woke up very early to a beautiful day. As Roy still seemed to be fast asleep I decided to go for a walk along the river before breakfast. Immediately I was met by a swarm of people of all ages out exercising. It seemed as if half of Brisbane was out walking, running, rowing or cycling. I saw young mums running with almost new-born babies in slings. One woman out for a run even had a small cart harnessed round her waist with an infant on board. I knew the country was sport mad, but here was some clear evidence of why Australian sportsmen and women are so often winners.

Australians love the outdoor life. Why wouldn't they? It is a beautiful country and the weather is wonderful. Men seem happiest when participating in sport or talking about it with their mates. However, from many conversations we had with local people, I did detect a possible downside to their sporting obsession. Whereas a young kid who loves participating in sport would thrive in Australian society I am not sure how a sensitive, bookish child would be regarded in a country with such a strong idolisation of sportsmen. In a conversation about this during our stay it was even suggested to me that non-sporty men fake enthusiasm in sport to avoid alienation.

On the whole we found Australians to be friendly and outgoing and easy to get along with. We experienced their friendliness first hand one evening returning home after the cricket. I think it was the third day of the match and we were walking from the Gabba to catch the river ferry. We had been deep in conversation with a group of Aussies about the game and continued to chat about it together when they reached their car and said their goodbyes. About 20 minutes later we looked up to check how close we were to the ferry and realised we were completely lost. This must have shown in our faces and behaviour because almost immediately two guys stopped their car and shouted over to us. One looked like a real city slicker whereas his pal was overweight with a rural look about him, his red chubby face adorned by a huge Stetson.

'Are you two boys okay? You look lost!' said the city man.

We confirmed that we were indeed lost and when we said we were heading for the ferry they both laughed.

'You're not only about an hour away, mate, you're also walking in the wrong direction. Where are you heading?' asked the city guy.

I replied that we usually caught the ferry at the Maritime Museum.

'No, he means where are you heading. Where would the ferry be taking you?' asked his farmer pal.

'Auchenflower,' Roy informed him.

City Man was even more amused. 'Christ mate, why do you want to go there?'

'It's where we are staying,' said Roy with no hint of shame despite City Man's suggestion that it was the back of beyond.

'It will be midnight before you get there,' he suggested. 'Get in!'

We hesitated. 'Do you want to go to bloody Auchenflower or not?' said the Stetson. It was not so much a question as an order to get in the car.

It would have seemed churlish and ungrateful to explain that we particularly enjoyed the ferry trip so we slid into the back seat and our two new friends proceeded at high speed towards Auchenflower.

It turned out that they were two old school mates who got together each year to watch cricket, but who since school had obviously followed different life paths. This mattered not a jot and the two of them indulged in light banter throughout the journey started by the Stetson objecting that the confounded car seat was wrapping itself around him.

'Is it getting warm?' City Man enquired, obviously revelling in his pal's discomfort.

'Warm?' he shrieked. 'Me bloody arse is on fire!'

'You must've activated the bubblebum device,' said City Man, obviously enjoying himself. 'It's to enhance your comfort. Everyone else loves it.'

'Bubblebum, my arse!' he yelled rather ingenuously. 'I don't see the point of a car like this. It wouldn't be much use for transporting sheep.'

City Man smiled to himself.

'So where are you two Poms from?' he asked, apparently bored with taking the piss out of his mate.

Roy, as is his way, answered the question in some detail and before long we were deep in conversation. City Man continued to propel his vehicle at an alarming speed and before we knew it we were back in Auchenflower.

Immediately we headed for the Regatta bar on the riverbank that had already been established as our local.

Australians love sitting outside having a few beers and I guess Australian beer suits their weather as well as their palate. However, for real ale lovers it was never going to hit the spot.

The beer was always served at a very low temperature so often the taste was frozen out. At the Regatta Inn we found a way around this. We soon developed the habit of ordering a jug with two glasses so that in the intense Australian heat it at least had a chance to warm up a bit before we drank it. However, every brand we tried, and we tried most of them, seemed to us to lack any real flavour. On the positive side, the beer was so strong we soon stopped thinking about the taste!

One evening at the Pig and Whistle, the Barmy Army HQ, Roy and I were, not for the first time, bemoaning the lack of ale when an Australian guy overheard us.

'You're just drinking the wrong stuff, boys. You need to drink the local brew!' he told us.

Was this salvation at last? Apparently unbeknown to us some master brewer, hidden from the view of tourists, was producing beer to die for right here in Brisbane. Eagerly we sought the identity of the ale in question.

'Just look up to heaven, mate!'

Our eyes followed his and there on the top of a very tall building, lighting up the night sky, was the immortal signature of the local brew: 'XXXX'. With a feeling of horror mixed with acute disappointment, we realised that the local brew of Brisbane was Castlemaine XXXX! We knew this stuff from home and neither of us could think of any beer that we liked less.

Likeable as they are, the Australians do not score highly on sense of humour. By that I am not wishing to imply that they do not like a laugh or a joke, because they clearly do. However, their understanding of the more subtle British humour is sadly lacking. At the end of the Brisbane Test England were on the end of a fierce drubbing. Nevertheless the England fans, led by the Barmy Army, continued to laugh and sing. When Billy Cooper, the Barmy Army's famous trumpeter put his instrument to his lips, the Australian fans did not know what to expect. As he gave a particularly plaintive rendition of 'The Last Post' the England fans fell about laughing while the Aussies looked on completely bemused.

Chapter Two

My Brother and Me

ROY WAS born two years before me. Soon he had reason to look back on that two-year period in which he was an only child as a golden epoch. Sitting in my high chair aged about ten months I announced myself by picking up a frying pan from the draining board and hitting him on the head, rendering him unconscious. He should have realised then that I would spell trouble for him. Instead, he spent our childhood as an exemplary older brother looking out for me in every way possible. As a result an otherwise peaceful and contented child continually found himself in scrapes not of his own making. On a domestic level this involved no more than taking the blame for the mess I continually made in our parents' much loved living room. Life outside was much more fraught.

Roy and I and a few of our local friends were avid train spotters which meant we spent a lot of time in the vicinity of the main line that went from London to Edinburgh right through our town. He had the train spotter's capacity to sit and wait, but I easily became bored. On one particular occasion we were sitting under a bridge supposedly waiting for the famous Mallard. The Mallard was the flagship engine for the Elizabethan Express which ran a non-stop service between London King's Cross and Edinburgh. As well as being a magnificent engine in its own right, the Mallard held the world record for the fastest speed ever reached by a steam locomotive, 126mph.

Roy and our pals regularly convinced themselves that the Mallard was about to pass through, but I had been disappointed more than enough times and no longer believed them. Trying to relieve the boredom of waiting, I suddenly came up with the idea of running across the railway line just before the train arrived. Our very sensible friends wanted none of it, but I was determined.

As I made my way down to the side of the track Roy became alarmed and followed me, fearing for my safety. When it became clear that I was intending to go through with it Roy made the decision to go with me to keep me safe. With Roy sweating and me laughing like a demented hyena, we ran across. Soon after the train passed through and as the smoke cleared we looked up to see the local bobby standing on the bridge. Several weeks later Roy appeared in the Magistrates' Court charged with trespass and was given a ticking off for leading his younger brother astray. I remained at home deemed 'below the age of criminal responsibility'.

In truth none of us were angels and there were a few occasions when we were marginally on the wrong side of the law, although we did not fully realise it at the time. A notable example was our 'recycling' of beer bottles for which in the 1950s and 60s there was always a deposit on return.

There was a strong Irish Catholic contingent in our part of town and on a Sunday morning under fear of death from their wives, not to mention the local priest, the men all dutifully attended Sunday Mass. As Mass concluded they left the church quietly showing due respect, but as they got a short distance away they picked up speed. As they rolled down the hill and into the pub known as the Gamekeeper, they resembled a herd of wildebeest in blue serge suits. They then drank solidly from noon until the pub closed at two, returning home in a shambolic state.

Later that afternoon beer crates were piled up at the back of the Gamekeeper inside the locked yard. While the landlord took a well-earned rest, our 'gang' gathered at the back of the yard outside the gate. As the youngest and smallest member I was inevitably nominated to climb over the metal gate and gather together armfuls of bottles, each with a thruppenny bit (three old pence) deposit on their head. I was lifted over the gate and I then handed the bottles through the railings to my co-conspirators. This left me with the problem of climbing back over without assistance which I invariably managed. Over the course of the next few days the older members of the group, Gerald Goodall, John Parsonage and my brother, returned the bottles and collected the deposits.

The suspicions of our parents were only raised if one of us was foolish enough to let them see the sweets we had bought with our ill-gotten gains. Our dads were paid on a Thursday and each of them returned home that evening with a selection of sweets for their kids; sherbet dips, spangles and jamboree bags were favourite. If you were seen sucking a gobstopper on a Tuesday or Wednesday it could only have been acquired illegitimately.

Whereas Roy was an amiable young lad, I loved nothing more than a good scrap. Unfortunately, I had a habit of starting fights with kids bigger and older than me. Driven by family loyalty and the knowledge that our mum would blame him if I got my head kicked in, Roy usually intervened.

Billy Vits was a level up. He lived around the corner from us and was known as the toughest boy in the neighbourhood.

He was three years older than me and built like a brick outhouse, but this did not deter me from picking a fight with him. When Roy discovered us squaring up to each other he told Billy to pick on someone his own size. To be fair, Billy had done everything he could to deter me, but Roy's challenge hit a raw nerve and my brother suffered a severe beating. I went home with my pride still intact but feeling a little bit guilty for the state of my brother's face.

As the years rolled on several things happened that made being my brother a little easier. Firstly, we went to different schools which meant that if I got myself into trouble, which I invariably did, I had to find my own way out of it. Secondly, team sports started to play a big part in our lives and given the age difference we pursued these separately.

Inevitably we began to develop different circles of friends and the amount of free time we spent together reduced as a result. The only leisure time we spent in each other's company was going to watch Chelsea with our dad or going to cricket matches. Nevertheless, Roy was always in the background lending a hand as and when required. It was he who persuaded the local newsagent to take me on as a paper boy although I was still underage and later I followed him into a series of part-time jobs culminating in working at the extremely chic Mecca dance hall.

Back on the home front he continued to rescue me from our parents' wrath on many occasions, most notably when they went out one evening and gave me permission to have some friends round for a 'party'. One of my best mates, John Finney, had become over-amorous with his girlfriend on a sofa bed in the living room resulting in the main wooden structure of the sofa cracking. Roy to the rescue. Before my parents had got home Fred, the joiner from the Mecca maintenance crew and a good friend of Roy's, had turned up and repaired it. When my parents returned the sight of a man ten years older than me sitting on the very same sofa enjoying a cup of tea was both reassuring and bewildering. Needless to say John Finney had long since cleared off.

Finally, Roy taught me to drive and together we purchased a red Morris Mini. It was a sort of 50/50 arrangement: I paid £50 and he paid the rest. We had clear rules governing our shared access to the car which Roy always stuck to and from which I continually sought exemptions. More often than not he gave way rather than suffer the hassle.

Our dad also played a big part in our lives and it was he who encouraged our love of sport, not only cricket and football, but also athletics and boxing.

Our dad was a massive fan of Muhammad Ali, not only because he was a great boxer, but also because he was so anti-establishment. Much to our mum's vexation dad was instantly attracted to anyone who kicked over the traces and Ali certainly did that. I have fond memories of the three of us glued to the radio in the early hours as the fights were broadcast live from Madison Square Garden in New York with electrifying commentary by the great Eamonn Andrews.

I later took up boxing and was pretty good. However, I probably took more punches than was necessary due to my insistence of boxing with my guard down as the great man was wont to do. Unfortunately, I wasn't quite as quick as he was!

Dad also influenced, or should I say determined, our politics and our view of the world. Thanks to him we developed strong social values believing firmly in the principles of social justice, freedom and mutual respect.

Even now when we go to watch cricket together we inevitably spend the first two hours discussing current affairs and putting the world to rights. Once that is done the conversation turns to the match we are at. It is one of the joys of cricket that you can have long conversations about any topic without missing any of the action. The conversation simply pauses as the ball is bowled and … instantly starts up again.

At the end of our second decade together I went off to university and Roy sought his fortune in the world of work. Although a good distance apart, we always kept in touch. It was only a matter of time until our family ties, our shared values and our love of cricket would inevitably draw us back together.

Chapter Three

Growing Up With Cricket

MY BROTHER has always been more interested in the past than the present. I do not know why this is. His main reading material is Charles Dickens novels and books about dead cricketers for whom he has a weird fascination. I do not mean cricketers that we watched as kids. I am talking about batsmen and bowlers who were famous long before we were born. While other cricket fans are queueing up for *No Spin: My Autobiography* by Shane Warne[2] or Jimmy Anderson's *Bowl. Sleep. Repeat.*[3] he is busy reading about the Bodyline series that took place in the early 1930s. I mean, we are both old enough to remember Richie Benaud as a player for goodness sake, so we can summon up enough cricketing history from our own memories.

As is often the case we got our passion for cricket from our father. He was never happier than when he was either watching cricket, playing it or teaching us the game.

When I was a kid we lived in a council house the size of a matchbox. Like most council houses built in the 50s it was well designed and functional. It was also quite spartan. The only source of heating was the open fire in the living room and except at weekends this was never lit until the evening.

My brother and I shared a bedroom above the living room and so the chimney breast continued through our room. So that our bedroom benefited from this construction there was a vent in the chimney breast at about eye level to allow any residual heat out. I don't have any recollection of luxuriating in the heat provided in this way. In fact I don't think it even stopped the bedroom windows from icing up on the inside!

The warm haven on school mornings was the kitchen. Our dad was always the first one up and his immediate task was to switch on the ancient fan heater in the kitchen to provide at least one warm room. The fan heater, known in the family as the 'blower heater', was a light brown metal box with a huge metal fan visible through the front grille. It stood on strong steel legs. It gave out considerable heat and by the time Roy and I got up and went into the kitchen it was already quite cosy.

The scene that met us was always the same. Our dad in his singlet stood at the kitchen sink shaving in front of a tiny mirror that swivelled on a blue plastic stand. The operation was facilitated by a whole array of facial distortions which never failed to make us smile. Recently we had our bathroom refurbished and for about a fortnight I had no mirror to shave by. One morning from goodness knows where my wife produced this self-same mirror. I was at first terrified to look into it as I expected my dad's face rather than mine to be looking back at me.

On the cooker stood a saucepan with a broken handle which was only ever used for porridge. The huge pot bubbled gently like a witch's cauldron, occasionally releasing hot plumes of sweet-smelling steam. The blower heater whirred noisily in the corner.

'In you come! Its warm in 'ere,' was the daily greeting.

Mind you, the size and comfort of the place we called home hardly mattered as we were always outside;

sometimes from choice, but more often driven out by our dad.

'What are you doing indoors?' was his first question on arriving home from work.

'It's raining, dad,' one of us would protest.

'It doesn't matter, it'll stop soon. Go on, get out!'

We were lucky in one respect. Our street and three others formed a square all backing on to a grassed area just big enough for a game of football or cricket. Also our mates from those streets, Ginger McNish, Arthur Garfield, John Casey, Gerald Goodall and many more, had dads who also believed in the outdoor life. As a result when we got turfed out into the rain our pals were there waiting for us.

However, our dad differed from theirs in one important respect. Not long after he had chucked us out he would appear himself, in winter with a couple of footballs and a whistle and in summer carrying a huge cricket bag of unknown vintage stuffed with bats, pads, stumps and gloves. The cricket ball he would carry separately, like some treasured artefact. In no time at all a proper game was underway as he directed us to the bizarrely named fielding positions of short leg, silly mid-on, backward point and into the covers. He only ever used the correct terms and only newcomers were given the luxury of a pointed finger or a gruff 'Over there!'

Here aged eight and ten respectively, kitted out in oversized cricketing clobber, we learned the game that was to become our passion. Neither of us were exceptional players, but cricket was and is everything to us and has remained so for more than half a century.

Even when the weather was just too bad to go out we were still obsessed with cricket. There is a very simple little game called 'Owzthat!' that is still sold today under the advertising slogan, 'The traditional cricket game for all weathers.' It consists of two hexagonal roller dice; one for the batsman with five scores on it and 'Owzthat!' on the sixth side. By rolling the dice each batsman in the team compiles a score until he throws 'Owzthat!' At that point the bowler rolls his dice with four sides rendering the batsman out, bowled, caught, stumped or lbw. On a fifth side he is saved by a no-ball and the sixth side gives him not out.

Money was very tight in our house and although this game probably only cost about five shillings my parents decided to make it themselves. My dad spent time at work making two short hexagonal metal bars and my mum typed out the numbers and phrases and stuck them on to the 'dice'. They were indestructible. Roy and I played this game for hours on end, sometimes compiling scores for whole Test series. We never argued about who should represent which team as I wanted to be England and he invariably wanted to be the West Indies.

Both Roy and I had aspirations to be pace bowlers, but Roy was better and faster than me with the appropriate physique to go with it. At first he modelled himself almost entirely on the Yorkshire and England legend, Fred Trueman, even developing a pigeon-toed approach to the wicket just like his hero. However, he soon had to abandon this strategy of impersonating Trueman as at the end of his 17-pace run-up, although 'fired up', he was almost too knackered to deliver the ball!

Our dad showed an interest in the progress of all of his charges, not just us two, and without doubt his most successful protégé was a thin blond lad called Colin (Paddy) Powell.

Paddy joined one of our games not knowing diddly-squat about cricket, but within three weeks became our star player. Over the years I have come across a few lads who seemed to excel at just about every sport and Paddy was certainly one of them. Following a trial I believe he was offered a junior contract at Middlesex County Cricket Club.

However, professional cricket was deprived of his talent as he chose football instead, going on to play 358 games for Charlton Athletic.

Compared to Paddy the rest of us had to huff and puff our way to success and with our dad's encouragement Roy and I both put in a lot of hard work which eventually brought its rewards.

Throughout our childhood, although money was short, we always had an annual summer holiday, usually in Cornwall. Everyone used cash in those days and at different locations around the kitchen was an array of tins and jars containing money put aside for various regular payments. There was a dried milk tin containing the rent, a jam jar with electricity money and an old-fashioned metal cash box containing the insurance money.

Dad was never a saver and so as the time of our holiday approached he would raid each tin or jar in turn to supplement the fortnight's wages he had been paid in advance until he thought we had enough to cover accommodation for two weeks in Cornwall. If he went as far as taking the insurance money we knew things were tight because this was collected each week by the Co-op insurance man, Mr Studland. Not having this particular pot of money therefore resulted in the added ignominy of having to hide under the kitchen table when he next called.

Mum on the other hand was a thrifty saver and often surprised dad by producing a wedge of money the day before we were due to set off. This extra cash was to be used for what was then known as 'luxuries'. If the money was not going to stretch to this we would get mum's famous speech on the first day away.

'Now, while we're away don't start asking dad for ice creams. If we can afford it, he'll get you one without being asked.'

It made good sense to us. We were in Cornwall and the sun was shining. We were already in heaven.

It was usually dad's choice to go to Cornwall. We were never certain whether dad chose that particular destination because of the scenery, beautiful beaches and reliable weather or whether he just thought the beaches made the best wickets offering some bounce for the seamers, especially when the tide was out.

As we all trekked across the huge beaches in search of hard, flat sand we looked like a squad of the Foreign Legion. Between the four of us we carried tennis rackets, windbreaks, a primus stove, a food hamper, a radio, deckchairs, buckets and spades and of course, bats, balls, and stumps!

Any thought of swimming or investigating rock pools had to wait until we had marked out our cricket pitch which had to be exactly the regulation 22 yards. Within an hour of our arrival dad had a game going with half the beach involved, adults and kids. If he noticed some lonely kid looking on he would immediately call him over and tell him he was batting next.

When Roy and I started taking holidays separate to our parents we were uncertain whether he missed our company or simply mourned the absence of a good 'length' bowler and a reliable extra cover.

We've had many wonderful cricketing experiences throughout our lives, but if we could re-live just one of them, high on the list would be playing cricket with dad on a beach in Cornwall.

Except when we were on holiday, every Saturday afternoon during the summer was spent at King George V Playing Fields watching our dad turn out for his firm's team.

They were captained by a portly chap, Ken Sykes, whose girth was almost equal to his height. In time-honoured manner he dispensed with the need for excessive running by despatching at least two balls every over to the boundary. I always thought his inability to run quick singles was on account of him being overweight, but he put it down to a shrapnel wound. Who was I to argue, especially as he was the best strokemaker in the team?

The wicketkeeper, Tom Buckle, also had a shape associated more with pork pies than press-ups. Tom was a stranger to cricket flannels, preferring army trousers held up by titanic braces. As a batsman he was a joy to watch with almost a full range of shots. I say 'almost' as I only remember him playing the sweep shot on one occasion when he needed the help of the slip cordon to get back up. When keeping wicket he took no interest in anything below his knees. As the ball whizzed past him, often conceding four byes, he would deflect any blame from himself by glaring menacingly at the bowler.

Possibly to divert attention from his own non-sporting figure the captain always referred to the number three batsman, James Pink, as 'Tubby' although he was no more than a stone overweight. Not particularly memorable as either a batsman or a fielder, the captain ensured Tubby Pink was the perpetual butt of team jokes.

Our mum was one of the wives whose duty was to prepare the afternoon tea where Ivy Lunnon's thick cut sandwiches and our mum's home-made Victoria sponge were the main attractions. It was lucky that the other players could invariably get to the pavilion before Ken and Tom. Once those two had filled their plates there were only meagre pickings for anyone who came later, often little more than sticks of celery and the garnish from the sandwiches.

Roy and I had the important job of scoring, using an ancient scorebook in which every detail of each player's batting and bowling performance was recorded each week along with the match result. As the game progressed nearly every player in turn would approach us with the same question.

'How many runs did I make?'

Almost all of them disputed the answer we gave them, usually maintaining that we had missed something crucial.

'I don't think you could've seen that on drive. It went for four, I'm sure it did!'

'You've got that down as byes. I got a bat on that, lad.'

'Not according to the umpire you didn't!' I would reply rather injudiciously.

'You need glasses, lad, like yer father!' was a typical riposte.

Roy, more sensible and less combative than me, was more likely to agree wholeheartedly with the indignant player but not actually make any alteration to the scorecard. As a result, he was seen as a team player whereas I was regarded as a nark or an arrogant upstart. Hardly surprising then that on that day of destiny when the team found themselves a man short it was Roy and not me that they turned to. Mind you at 14 he was already taller than most of them and so looked the part to play in a men's team. I was just an underweight argumentative little squirt. However, I maintain to this day he was not picked because he was a better player than me.

Looking back to this time it was normal for any decent-sized firm to have their own cricket and football team. Often the firm you worked for operated as a type of community. Each week employees made a voluntary contribution directly from their wages into the company sports and social club and this was supplemented by the employer. The football and cricket teams were funded from this source. I am sure in other parts of the country other sports prevailed, for example rugby league in certain northern towns.

The bigger the firm the more teams there were and the wider the variety of sports offered. Sports and social clubs attached to larger companies might offer rugby, football, archery, tennis, shooting, bowls, sailing, angling, badminton and other indoor sports, but always cricket. There were also social events like Christmas and New Year dances. The children of the employees benefited as well from this system with occasional trips in the summer and at Christmas a party for the little ones and a pantomime outing for the older children. It is noteworthy that irrespective of their interest in sport almost all employees joined the sports and social club and contributed willingly. Happy days!

There are still some examples today of workplace sports and social clubs which operate on this model, but many of the old clubs that have survived have floated free from the employer and now look to sources like the lottery for their funding.

Following his unexpected call-up to dad's firm's team Roy continued to get opportunities to play and by the time he left school he was turning out regularly for them. He was a good player and eventually progressed to playing for the town second XI. However, by his early 20s he had pretty well given up playing, having found the upper-class prejudicial atmosphere of the club unbearable. Instead he put his energies into building up his china and glass business and just playing the occasional village game.

The difference between the large and well-established cricket club that my brother found himself in and the firm's team where he had played with our dad could not be more stark. As far as Ken Sykes, Tubby Pink and indeed our dad were concerned cricket was the people's game to be enjoyed by everybody irrespective of background, sporting ability or class. The club that Roy joined had very different origins. Founded and run by lawyers, magistrates and wealthy local dignitaries, the club was more interested in a player's background than his ability with a cricket ball. A big, strong, working-class lad was of little interest to them however fast he could bowl.

The other cricket played when I was a young man was village cricket based around the local pub but originally almost certainly organised by the village church or chapel. During the second half of the 19th century religion and cricket came together with the formation of church and chapel teams.

Such an eventuality had seemed remote during the first half of that century with clergymen opposed to, even fearful of, popular sports. Why clerical attitudes changed allowing churches, chapels and Sunday schools to form cricket clubs is not entirely clear. However, the most likely explanation is that chapels in particular brought together rural working men and the development of shared sporting activities naturally followed from this.

My early memories of first-class cricket saw these various strands of the game at odds with each other. Slowly county cricket, at the time still administered by members of the establishment, had to find a way of accommodating working class 'professionals' because that was where the talent lay. I am glad now to witness first-class cricket and in particular English cricket at peace with itself where talent is the only serious criterion for selection.

Chapter Four

Back in the Saddle

ROY AND I had put a brave face on it, but in truth we had been badly bruised by the result in Australia at the beginning of 2007. We had headed to Brisbane at the end of 2006 full of hope and expectation only to see the first of five Test defeats at the hands of the old enemy. However, they say that if you are thrown from a horse you should quickly get back in the saddle and so we had acquired tickets for the second and third Tests against the West Indies, England's first series since the 5-0 Ashes defeat.

A rain-affected first Test at Lord's had ended in a draw and we were hoping for a more positive result in the second Test at Headingley.

In 2007 my daughter Emily and her husband Andy were living in Leeds where Emily was a PhD student. They had bought a large Victorian terrace house with plenty of room for Roy and I to stay.

The other advantage was that Emily had become a Yorkshire member and so for once we could leave the responsibility for acquiring the tickets to someone else. We had tickets for the first four days.

The match was due to start on Friday, 25 May and so Roy and I landed at Emily's from our different starting points early on Thursday evening. As one might expect we spent the evening in a local pub getting ourselves in the right frame of mind for the game.

The ground was about a mile and a half from their house so we decided to set off relatively early to walk there.

Roy's puffy ankles had been a significant factor in our trip to Australia, often slowing our progress as we explored Brisbane, but he had always put the excessive swelling down to the long flight. A brief visual inspection as he was getting dressed that morning reassured me that his ankles were now in good order so I was surprised when on the walk to Headingley he began to fall behind.

Prior to moving to Leeds, Emily and Andy had spent about seven years living in London. Like lots of young people in the capital they did not own a car, preferring to get around by walking or travelling on the Tube. As a result the two of them were used to walking at a very brisk rate. Roy on the other hand liked to saunter, observing the city and its people, at a leisurely speed.

Emily thinks the world of her 'Uncle Roy'. He and his family had featured large in Emily's childhood and their relationship had been further cemented through our shared experiences of the 2005 Ashes. Despite this, she was not averse to a little gentle ribbing of her uncle as an 'old git' who walked slowly and was always dressed for winter. I have to confess that I was guilty of encouraging this as it allowed me to present myself as the younger, fitter brother.

However, on this occasion something else was at play and I was probably to blame. When walking somewhere with Emily I was always telling her to slow down whereas with Roy I usually complained that we would never get where we were going if he did not speed up a bit. Both

Roy and Emily objected in their own way. Each of them has a stubborn streak and on this occasion it was being demonstrated by their unwillingness to compromise their pace of walking.

Soon I had a real problem on my hands as the gap between Emily, Andy and Roy grew to several hundred yards. I had placed myself between them in an attempt to stay in touch, but it was not working. Emily and Andy had disappeared round one corner whereas Roy was just about emerging from a street behind me. Finding the ground would not be a problem as everyone was heading in that direction, but Emily had our tickets.

In those days neither Roy nor I had developed the habit of always carrying a mobile and so I saw difficulties ahead in relocating my errant daughter. I did at least know Emily's number which had not changed in years so I accosted some young guy and virtually demanded the use of his phone. He looked me up and down, taking particular note of my tense, strained expression and concluded I was at the very least eccentric, possibly dangerous, and handed it over. I had almost mastered how to make a call from this guy's space-age phone when Emily suddenly arrived on the scene. At the same time Roy, having independently realised he had no ticket, appeared red-faced from the opposite direction, but thankfully too out of breath to complain.

Emily took the phone from me and passed it to the young man with no word of thanks nor even the faintest acknowledgement, rather like someone passing the baton in a relay race having unexpectedly found themselves in last place. The young man scuttled quickly away, convinced that his original diagnosis of me as a potentially dangerous psychopath applied to the whole family. Twenty minutes later we were all seated waiting for the match to start as if nothing had happened.

If we wanted any reassurance that the Test team had recovered their equilibrium after the recent Ashes debacle then the England batsmen certainly provided it. Michael Vaughan, thankfully reinstated as captain, scored an excellent hundred and Kevin Pietersen ended the day on 130 not out. England, especially Pietersen, had been flying and were 366/5 at the close.

On the second day Pietersen carried on where he had left off. Ably supported by Matt Prior and then Liam Plunkett with a flurry of shots, Pietersen was last man out for 226. England declared between lunch and tea on 570/7.

The rest of the day was disastrous for the West Indies. At tea they were two wickets down in their first innings and at the close, having followed on, were two wickets down in their second innings facing almost certain defeat.

For the England fans the atmosphere was electric. As Pietersen tore into the West Indies attack the crowd went mad. With an array of fancy-dress outfits and the Barmy Army in full voice in the Western Terrace there was a real party atmosphere, for many of us a release from the trauma of the recent Ashes tour.

Overnight some awful weather set in and by the morning it was pouring with rain and the temperature had fallen significantly. The summer party of the previous day had been replaced by a distinctly autumnal feeling. The whole day was rained off but given how close we were to the ground we never left home.

On Monday morning we got up to find that the temperature had fallen further and a misty rain was blowing across the city. More in hope than expectation we set off for the ground. If the weather forecast was to be believed we would at least see some cricket.

According to the BBC it was the coldest ever Test match day. The BBC held it to be 7.4°C at the start of play, lower than the 8°C that was recorded when England played New Zealand at Edgbaston in 1965. For a short while it actually snowed!

Brought up playing cricket in the Caribbean sun, this must have been a real shock to the system for the West Indies team and there was every indication that they were simply not interested in playing in these arctic conditions.

One after another they trooped out wearing three or four jumpers and soon after headed back to the warmth of the pavilion with very few runs to their name. Only Dwayne Bravo showed any resistance with a defiant half-century including seven fours and a six.

We were all wearing overcoats and hats and were still cold. After several rain breaks and just 33 overs bowled on the fourth day the misery finally came to an end with the West Indies all out for 141. The British weather at its historic worst, with a little help from the England bowlers, had predictably induced the West Indies' heaviest defeat by an innings and 283 runs. By the time the West Indies surrender was complete the temperature had probably crept up to about nine degrees.

To the West Indians it was about as much fun as Estonian ice cricket, which holds its annual world championship on Harku Lake in Tallinn. If the weather conditions are just too bad the games are moved to an ice rink in an old Soviet missile factory. Teams consist of six players with rolling substitutes so the normal squad number is between six and ten. If you play outside, the wicket is painstakingly carved out of the ice and the boundary marked off to keep the bewildered locals off the outfield. The boundaries are either snow-banks or are patrolled by officials on ice skates; if you strike a skater an extra six runs is added to your score.

Each year cricket teams from all over the world descend on Estonia's beautiful capital city, with grand plans and strategies to conquer the conditions in the hope of winning the tournament, only to be beaten by a team of no-hopers. So far the West Indies have not entered the competition.

* * *

Barry is a good friend from a nearby village who I often enjoy a pint with. He is retired now, but was a travelling salesman for many years dealing with forklift trucks and similar machinery. However, his passion was always training Labrador retrievers which he has done for many years along with his wife. We have two dogs ourselves and he is a fount of knowledge on all dog training issues.

About 20 years ago Barry started to show an interest in cricket, especially Test cricket. He had never played the game other than at school, but like many people became fascinated through listening to *Test Match Special*.

The beguiling commentaries have hooked many a non-cricket fan over the years as the team spend as much time discussing the wine that went with last night's dinner as the cricket. This is not to suggest they lack sharpness. On the contrary, when the match demands it they will describe the action in precise detail, but if the cricket is flagging they will turn their thoughts to other things: the quality of cake that listeners have sent in or the state of London buses. Then effortlessly they can return to the action in front of them. It is recognised by many as a unique presentation style.

Soon Barry was watching the matches, or at least the highlights, on television and was always wanting to discuss the state of the game when we met in the local pub. This of course suited me perfectly.

In 2007 I found myself with two tickets for the Saturday of the third Test at Old Trafford. Originally Roy and I were planning to go together, but he had now jibbed. Having frozen to death at Headingley at the end of May I don't think he wanted to risk the northern weather again just ten days later. After a little thought I decided to offer the spare ticket to Barry.

He had never been to watch a professional cricket match before and immediately jumped at the chance to accompany me. He was in fact very keen indeed and I was pleased that I had invited him. I picked him up at about nine on the morning of the match and we set off to Manchester. It soon became clear that I should have asked Barry to drive.

Although I had driven to Old Trafford umpteen times I chose this occasion to go wrong.

'Are we lost?' he asked with a deadpan face.

'Not really,' I replied. 'I have gone wrong somewhere, but I think I know where I am. Why, which way would you go from here?'

Of course, he had spent almost his whole working life driving around North Wales and the North West of England.

'I wouldn't have come this way in the first place,' he said and that was all the help I was going to get.

Luckily I did find my way to the ground, but I read Barry's silence as a sign that he would have chosen a better route. C'est la vie. We arrived at about 10.30am, still in plenty of time for the start of play.

As we entered the ground Barry's adventure of watching live Test cricket began in earnest as the bag search relieved him of his four cans of beer. His complaints were ignored as the steward simply passed on to the next person in line.

'Why didn't you tell me you weren't allowed to bring drinks in?'

'You are, lemonade in plastic bottles,' I replied with an ironic smile.

Barry was not impressed. 'I'm not going to get pissed on that, am I?'

'Don't worry, you can replace them at the bar. It'll only cost you 16 pounds.'

After a short while we found our seats. Barry sat down and I went off to fetch two coffees. I returned just in time to hear the strains of 'Jerusalem'.

'Bloody hell, these seats are hard. If you'd told me I would have brought a cushion,' he complained with a hard stare towards a spectator in front of us who had a double cushion supporting his back as well as his rump.

'Once the cricket starts you won't notice,' I told him with little confidence that this would prove to be so. 'They're coming out now.'

The two umpires had emerged followed by the West Indies side, each of whom seemed consumed with their own pre-match exercises. Some were running backwards while others were touching their toes. The two opening bowlers were swinging their arms in wide arcs. Eventually they formed a huddle, allowing the skipper to give his customary last-minute pep-talk. As they took up their fielding places Michael Vaughan and Alastair Cook skipped across the boundary line on their way to the square. Finally, Barry seemed quite excited.

Soon the cricket was underway and Cook and Vaughan were going well until, just two short of their century partnership, Vaughan gave a sharp chance back to the bowler, Daren Sammy. It was a straight drive hit hard, but just in the air, allowing Sammy to take a great reaction catch in his follow-through, grabbing the ball with his right hand.

Cook was joined by Kevin Pietersen and at once the pace picked up.

At lunch England were 136/2 having added over a hundred runs in the morning session.

Both Barry and I had brought a lot of food with us, but before we started our lunch I suggested we have a pint at the bar. Roy and I rarely drink during a county game, but we have a tradition of a couple of pints at lunchtime during a Test match. However, Barry would have none of it. I assumed he was still smarting from the confiscation of his four cans of beer and that I had further put him off by mentioning the prices.

Any casual observer who has witnessed the inebriated, albeit good-humoured crowd at Test matches in England will realise that the price of ale does little to deter most people from filling their boots. Nevertheless, it is a fact that beer prices at cricket grounds in this country are outlandishly high. Having watched cricket in Sri Lanka, Australia and South Africa where the prices are very similar to what you would pay in the city, I see no excuse for the ramping up of prices that takes place here.

Having said that, I did want a pint, but Barry remained firmly in his seat. Going for a beer on my own is not my idea of fun so I opened my lunch box and selected a slice of spinach and roasted tomato quiche to start. Reluctantly, I opened a small carton of orange juice and took a resentful swig.

After lunch Cook and Pietersen continued to bat well, sharing a partnership of 122 until Pietersen was out hit wicket in the most unusual circumstances. A sharp bouncer from Dwayne Bravo took Pietersen totally by surprise, knocking his helmet off which then fell on to his stumps.

As we waited for Paul Collingwood to join Cook I asked Barry if the game was living up to his expectations.

'It's been enjoyable, especially while Pietersen was in, but the bugger's out now,' he said, almost implying that was it. I made no comment.

After tea Alastair Cook reached his century, but that was followed by an all too familiar England batting collapse from 265/3 to 313 all out. Debutant Daren Sammy finished with incredible figures of 7-66. Nevertheless, England had still set the West Indies a formidable target of 455 runs to win.

With just eight overs left in the day we decided to make a move. Old Trafford is a difficult ground to get away from and we hoped that by leaving half an hour early we would avoid the worst of the traffic.

Back in the car I asked Barry for his final assessment of the day out.

'The trouble is I can't see the ball,' he told me.

We had been sitting behind the bowler's arm and most of the day the medium-paced Daren Sammy or occasionally Dwayne Bravo had been bowling from one end with the spinners rotating from the other. I might have understood if the opening bowlers, Fidel Edwards and Jerome Taylor had been on, they were seriously fast, but they bowled very little.

'Do you think you need new glasses?' I asked.

'They're fine when I watch on telly,' he said. 'I'll probably just do that in future. Anyway, my armchair is much more comfortable than those plastic seats. My backside is still hurting now.'

Well, from my point of view there was very little else to be said.

I did not have a ticket for day four but watched the highlights at home and was able to witness a spirited fightback from the West Indies. They lost only four wickets in the day and at close had reached 301/5. Except for the captain, Daren Ganga who was out for a duck, the whole top and middle order contributed led by the great run machine Shivnarine Chanderpaul. The West Indies were chasing a daunting target of 455, but suddenly it seemed possible. The final day was going to be well worth watching.

CRICKET, MY BROTHER AND ME

So the last day of the match began with England needing five wickets for victory and the West Indies requiring a further 154 runs. England remained favourites, but with Chanderpaul still at the crease it was far from plain sailing.

I was at the time working as assistant director for the children's charity Barnardo's and very conveniently I discovered that I had a meeting scheduled for 9.30am with the service manager of one of Barnardo's Manchester-based services. Jack was himself a massive sports fan and I had no difficulty in telling him that I intended to go straight to the cricket once the meeting was concluded. As a result he cooperated fully in sticking to the agenda so that I could leave before 11. There was little doubt that he was considering coming too and it would only have taken a word from me for him to do just that.

Before I worked for Barnardo's I worked for social services in a Merseyside authority for 27 years. I had started as a basic grade social worker and had worked my way up to a senior position. Inevitably I made a lot of friends during that time, many of whom remained working on the ground with me as their boss. There were numerous occasions when this created difficulties for everyone and I had resolved when I joined Barnardo's that I would steer away from forming personal relationships with staff.

Jack was a similar age to me with the same politics and many of the same interests. Had I met him in a different sort of setting I have no doubt we would have become good friends. I thought about inviting him, but with only the briefest hesitation I took my leave and headed for Old Trafford. It would just have been too complicated, particularly for him.

There was only a small fifth-day crowd and so gaining admission was straightforward and inexpensive. I arrived just in time to see wicketkeeper/batsman Denesh Ramdin get out. He appeared surprised by the extra bounce from a Monty Panesar delivery and was caught at first slip by the ever-reliable Paul Collingwood. 311/6.

The small crowd was not perfect for me as I should have been in work and the chances of being caught on camera were higher than in a full house. I had already decided to work a few extra hours to make up the time but being seen would still be an embarrassment. I resolved to keep any celebrations muted so as not to attract any attention from the cameras. Then, acting like some second-rate gangster incognito, I pulled my cap down and my collar up, thereby making myself a perfect target for any bored cameraman.

Chanderpaul was now joined by all-rounder Daren Sammy, whose exploits with the ball on day three had set up this game. He was playing well while at the other end Chanderpaul just batted on, but on 25 Sammy hit a fearsome straight drive back towards the bowler and Panesar, hardly renowned for his fielding, took a great return catch. 348/7.

Although Chanderpaul continued to resist, the tail contributed little and Steve Harmison and Monty finished the job in the fifth over after lunch with the West Indies still 60 short of their target.

I returned to work feeling reasonably satisfied with the result. However, although England's victory by 60 runs gave them an unassailable 2-0 lead in the series it was clear that the West Indies were not strong opposition. Roy and I had targeted this series to try and ascertain whether the England team had returned to full health following the 5-0 debacle that we had partially witnessed in Australia at the turn of the year.

In truth few conclusions could be drawn from this series. It was good to see the captain Michael Vaughan back and in reasonably good form, but it was hard to say whether England were firmly on the road to recovery.

Chapter Five

Playing Cricket: Our Rise to the Bottom

AS WAS the norm back then, our first introduction to competitive cricket was at school. Roy and I had gone our separate ways in terms of schooling with Roy attending the local secondary modern while I got a place at a posh grammar school boasting centuries of cricket excellence. However, this went in his favour rather than mine as Roy was assured of a regular place in the cricket team for his entire school career while I struggled to make the first team given the cricketing talent that surrounded me.

My eventual 'breakthrough' came in the most unusual of circumstances. As one of only two pupils from a council estate I quickly developed a pugnacious attitude in order to survive any attempts to single me out for bullying and in this I was very successful, usually leaving my tormentors the worse for wear. Unfortunately, and largely to my detriment, I maintained this attitude with regard to school discipline. I must have come across as a difficult and antagonistic pupil at times. I certainly broke all records in terms of corporal punishment and frequency of detentions. I often ended up with detention on a Saturday morning, the school having exhausted every other means of punishment available.

On one such Saturday I found myself as the only pupil in a large classroom completing some miserable and pointless piece of work while an unfortunate young teacher was forced to waste part of his own weekend supervising me. Suddenly and unexpectedly the door opened and Mr Williams, the deputy head, entered the room.

'For God's sake, not Hart again!' he said disdainfully. 'You get off home to your family, Mr Nichols. Leave Hart to me.'

Mr Nichols was not about to look a gift horse in the mouth and was soon out of the room. Mr Williams turned to address me.

'Have you got your cricket gear in school?' he asked with an air of urgency.

'Yes, sir, it's all in my locker, but it's pretty dirty from the House match on Thursday.'

Under normal circumstances turning out in dirty kit would have resulted in immediate dismissal from the field of play, but these were apparently not normal circumstances.

'Never mind that, go and get changed and get yourself over to the cricket pitch. The first team are a man short.'

'I will, sir, but you do realise I'm a fourth year? I'm only just 15.'

Mr Williams looked at me with a mixture of bewilderment and impatience.

'Of course I know how old you are, you stupid arse. Do you want to play or would you rather finish your detention?'

'I'm desperate to play, Mr Williams,' I assured him.

'Then look lively!'

As I ran off towards the changing rooms to get my kit he called after me with what he thought were words of encouragement but sounded to me more like a threat.

'And don't let the school down, Hart. Just remember what I always tell you: "line and length".'

Mr Williams was one of those people that every school needs. He was an absolute stalwart, the glue that held the school together. He taught maths and was nominally the deputy head in charge of the lower school, but in reality he pretty much ran the place. More often than not he took morning assembly with the headmaster only putting in an appearance when there was something grave to impart like defeat in an important rugger match.

He also presided over both lunchtime sittings in the ancient dining hall, leading the boys in a recital of Grace in Latin. The room was brought to order by Mr Williams pressing a plunger on an antique brass bell. The high-pitched ring of the bell was briefly followed by complete silence before being replaced by the sound of several hundred chairs being scraped back as every boy stood to attention. Then Mr Williams' solo voice rang out.

'Benedictus.'

Following Mr Williams' introduction, we all lustily sang the words of the opening Grace.

'Benedictus, Benedicat, per Jesum Christum Dominum Nostrum Amen.'

Then we sat down as one and tucked into an excellent lunch.

Most importantly Mr Williams, despite the school having a full-time PE teacher, organised all team sports and turned out himself to referee rugby matches and umpire the games of cricket. He probably put in more hours on extra-curricular activities than teaching maths. Much to the chagrin of opposition teams, he was infamous for coaching his own side from his advantageous position of referee or umpire.

During a cricket match he would sit on a shooting stick wearing his white coat and cap and, as the bowler returned to his mark, offer advice on how to bowl the next ball. It was from this vantage point that he again repeated his 'line and length' mantra as I came on to bowl my debut over.

The school first team was made up largely of boys in the fifth form and lower sixth with just one or two fourth years who were exceptionally talented. For me it was a huge step up. Had I been selected in the normal way to play in the exalted first team then at this point I would have been as nervous as a kitten but given how the opportunity had been unexpectedly thrust upon me I did not have time to worry. I just marked out my run and bowled, as instructed on a good line and at a fullish length. The result was that I took three wickets and helped my team to victory. However, to put the win in context the school had not lost a match for nearly three years. Still, the performance held me in good stead, and I pretty well held my place from that point, although I always felt that my position in the team was rather tenuous.

Meanwhile Roy's school career, as a cricketer but alas not as an academic, was flourishing. He had become a reliable and reasonably fast bowler and a tidy right-hand bat and was an automatic selection for the school team, but then there was Andy Bell.

Given that Andy Bell was a good friend of Roy's it would seem inappropriate to refer to him as my brother's nemesis, but he was a sort of pain in the side for Roy, a constant reminder of what he could not quite achieve.

Andy was a stocky, squarely built lad who only played cricket because Roy, as a passionate lover of the game, had persuaded him to give it a try. He had never proclaimed any particular liking for the game and in truth this did not change even when he became so successful. Roy had worked his socks off to reach a decent standard as a bowler whereas Andy had never studied the art, practised in the nets or given his technique any real thought. He would not have been able to name more than two England players, if that.

Nevertheless, he could bowl accurately on a good length and achieve blistering pace. He never marked out a run-up, he changed from over the wicket to round without knowing why and sometimes released the ball from a metre behind the line, but he was dynamite.

It was difficult for Roy, but he came to accept that some youngsters just had an abundance of natural talent. In the end he was just glad that Andy was bowling in tandem with him rather than firing down hand grenades for the opposition. We had seen it as kids with Paddy Powell, who I mentioned earlier. Like Andy he took to the game with such ease and developed incredibly quickly. As with most youngsters who love sport Roy and I had to put in the hard yards, but we did it willingly.

It was interesting to compare how our relative matches were organised. In my case we had a typed fixture list covering the whole season. Our opponents were largely teams from other private grammar schools, and we travelled to away games in a coach wearing full school uniform. Like us, most schools we visited had a pavilion where we enjoyed a very civilised afternoon tea at the change of innings.

In Roy's case, although he got to play competitive cricket for the whole summer, he never knew who their next opponents were. They could be inter-house matches, first XI versus second XI or games against other schools. Often after school I would see dad piling Roy and all the local kids into his Ford Consul to take on other schools and various scratch sides. Often they would return with tales of local estate rivalry resulting in punch-ups at the end of or even during matches. I often wished I could be part of it. In our school matches we played a high standard of cricket, but it was all so sanitised.

At 18 I went off to university where I played a few games while Roy got a succession of local jobs. After leaving school he continued to play for dad's firm's team. Dad sometimes turned out too, but ironically usually offered to be the scorer, the role that Roy and I had undertaken as kids. I sometimes played alongside them during college holidays, which we all enjoyed immensely.

Inevitably there was a slow changing of the guard with most players from the firm's team we had known as kids now watching us play. The team was still very ably led by captain Ken Sykes, whose figure was now beyond being described as 'portly'. However, he could still bat. The wicketkeeper, Tom Buckle, had finally reached the point where any form of crouching was beyond him and had passed his gloves to a younger and considerably slimmer man.

The team now consisted of a number of sons of former players, most notably Michael Lunnon whose dad Joe had played with our father. His mother Ivy I have alluded to before as the curator of thick-cut cheese and ham sandwiches for the tea. Michael could bowl at the speed of light and was playing well below the level that would have been appropriate to his skills. However, he enjoyed it and the rest of us certainly enjoyed having him there, unlike the opposition.

Although we still played under the firm's banner the organisation of inter-works competitions was already starting to break down and more often than not we found ourselves playing village teams of which there were many.

One ground sticks in my mind. On this small Hertfordshire village green the cricket square was immaculate. However, from the roadside end the outfield fell away alarmingly so anyone with a good straight drive in their armoury was guaranteed a boundary as soon as the ball passed the bowler.

Of course, some poor fool had to bowl from this end, struggling up the hill to reach the wicket. The job for the home side usually fell to the local blacksmith. He was a brute of a man with red hair and an even redder face, especially when bowling from the roadside end as the sheer exertion would inevitably manifest itself in his complexion. He was genuinely fast and could make the ball swing both ways. However, the opportunity to look at his grip to try and ascertain whether he was bowling the out-swinger or a straight-on delivery was denied you. As he approached up the hill, for a long time you could see nothing but his red hair and florid face. Then suddenly his mighty frame would materialise before your eyes. Racked with fear, the last thing on your mind was to concentrate on his wrist action. Staying alive seemed a greater priority.

* * *

Later in life when I was a social worker I played regularly for the social services team in knockout matches and friendlies organised by our trade union. I was an all-rounder of the sort who was not quite good enough as either a batsman or a bowler but was worth my place because I could do a bit of each. Nowadays I would be given the rather unflattering title of a 'bits and pieces' player.

I recall one occasion when we were playing a friendly against Liverpool Schools, represented by teachers from a number of local educational institutions. Having had a few good games where I had been amongst the wickets, I was invited to open the bowling. As I stood waiting to bowl I nervously went through the warm-up routines that I had seen my heroes perform on the telly. Finally, the two opening batsmen approached the square. Imagine my surprise when I realised that the guy who was to face the first ball, Ewen, was a close friend with whom we had lived in Liverpool. Since moving across the Mersey to live and work I had seen less of him. However, I did recall that his father Peter Arnold, a Kiwi by birth, was a professional cricketer who had opened the batting for Northamptonshire County Cricket Club for the best part of ten years.

As soon as we spotted each other the competitive juices began to flow. Ewen had a wry smile on his face but did not in any way acknowledge me. With a sudden rush of adrenalin, I delivered the first ball faster than I thought possible and it whizzed past his ears. Our wicketkeeper took two paces back. Ewen was ready for the next delivery and calmly leaned away and hooked it to the boundary. The third delivery was given the same treatment. The next ball he drove for four and followed this with a straight six back over my head. As I walked briskly back to my mark I was feeling pretty angry, but not as angry as our captain who was fielding at mid-off. He was obviously regretting his decision to allow me to bowl the first over.

'Try bowling at the bleedin' stumps!' was all he said as I passed.

I ran in at a ferocious pace and gave a primitive cry as Ewen's middle stump cartwheeled out of the ground. He had already scored 18 off the over, but I still felt that I had come out on top, although this feeling was later tempered by the fact that we lost by almost a hundred runs!

When I was in my late 40s and had not played any cricket for some time I was persuaded, against my better judgement, to bowl for the local village team. I went to pre-season nets and practised by bowling to my daughter Emily in one of our fields. Although the field bore no relation to a cricket pitch in that it was dangerously uneven, she stood up with great stoicism.

Eventually the big day came and I was asked to bowl first change. My first delivery bounced twice and the second one was a beamer, passing the batsman's head without bouncing. I had been bowling well in the nets, but now suddenly I did not seem to know when to release the ball. The next few deliveries I bowled really slowly and although they were harmless and innocuous I did get through the over. The captain was not sure what to do so I made the decision for him. For the first time in my life I had the 'yips', only too familiar to bowlers and golfers, and I was not going to bowl another over. By unspoken, but mutual consent, I never played for them again.

I do firmly believe that fast bowling, which is essentially about rhythm, is the hardest cricketing skill to maintain when you have not been playing for a long time. As if to emphasise this point, at about the same time Roy had a similar experience, although he struggled with line rather than length. He bowled two or three overs, but never really got his line right and decided to call it a day. It seemed the time had come to allow our prowess as players to be replaced by the joy of watching the game.

Chapter Six

Our First Test Match

IN FACT, thanks to our dad, we had been watching first-class cricket from an early age as well as playing the game. For our first ever match he aimed high and took us to Lord's, the most famous cricket ground in the world. It was 1963 and England were playing the West Indies at the start of the period in which the Windies would dominate international cricket.

They were captained by the legendary Frank Worrell, who two years earlier had become the first black cricketer to captain a West Indian team on tour when he led them in Australia. A week earlier they had annihilated England in the first Test at Old Trafford. Their side also included possibly the greatest ever all-rounder, Garfield Sobers, who already held the record for the highest Test score of 365. Many decades later I spotted him sitting in the stands at Trent Bridge, the home of Nottinghamshire County Cricket Club, looking for all the world like an average person rather than the super-hero he really was.

Wes Hall and Charlie Griffith were the first of many fearsome opening bowling partnerships from the West Indies. During the next 20 years the Caribbean would produce many more. To Roy and I these people were the faces on playing cards that we collected avidly. And here they were suddenly appearing before us in the flesh. When we saw Hall and Griffith bowling we were awestruck by the unbelievable speeds at which they propelled the ball.

After seeing these two at work Roy temporarily returned to his 17-pace run-up, but as before the detrimental effect on his stamina was more significant than any benefit to his bowling.

The match is remembered because England batsman, Colin Cowdrey, his arm broken earlier by a fearsome delivery from Wes Hall, came out to bat at the end of the match with his arm in plaster and helped save the game.

For my brother and me the game is remembered for a different reason. In those days even at Lord's you could sit on the grass behind the boundary rope to watch the match and this is what we were doing. On the day you could hire cushions to make the long vigil slightly more comfortable and most spectators took advantage of this.

We were sitting innocently watching the cricket when our dad was struck on the back of the head by a flying cushion. His glasses fell off, sending him into a rage.

Our mum had often told us about the times before they were married when he would suddenly lose his temper with complete strangers.

These stories were fascinating to us as we only knew him as a mild-mannered fellow who appeared not to have a temper at all! Despite the many times that I in particular had tried his patience he never responded angrily and throughout our childhood he rarely if ever laid a glove on us, unusual for the time.

I especially remember mum's story about him threatening to punch some bloke's lights out because he had pushed her in a bus queue! And here he was, only 5ft 8in in his stockinged feet and a good two stone over his best fighting weight, confronting four enormous West Indian spectators.

'Which one of you threw that bloody cushion?' he demanded.

At first they tried to pass it off as a joke, but finding that this tactic was infuriating him even more, opted for a full apology. Thankfully he accepted it gracefully and our fears that our dad would be taken home in an ambulance finally subsided.

I understand how my dad felt at the time. Scrabbling about on the grass for his spectacles, he felt humiliated, but I am sure now that he was wrong in thinking it was a hostile act. All the West Indian supporters around us were very raucous in support of their team and chucking cushions in the air was just part of their exuberant celebrations. And wow, did they have something to celebrate! We were approaching lunch on the second day. The West Indies had completed their first innings scoring just over 300 and now paceman Charlie Griffith had dismissed the two renowned England openers, Edrich and Stewart, for nought and two respectively.

A West Indies cricket team that had the ability to beat England was a big deal for the immigrants from the Caribbean. West Indians had come to Britain in pursuit of a better life, but any hopes that this country would prove to be a paradise for residents of its former colonies were soon dispelled.

From the beginning people from the Caribbean who came to the British Isles often faced a hostile reception as well as verbal and sometimes physical violence from racist groups. This became particularly intense in the 1960s and 1970s. Hence the West Indies cricket team became an inspiration for black Britons in these trying times. West Indian victory was all the more sweet when it took place in front of crowds of West Indian migrants who used cricket to make a statement against the racism they encountered in their adopted home. From their days of slavery to contemporary racism they had been exploited and abused. Now, at least on the cricket field, it was the turn of the white man to have their collective arses kicked!

From that day on Roy became a complete devotee of Caribbean cricket with its aggressive pace bowling, free flowing yet powerful batting and agile, athletic fielding. Being that bit younger I found it hard to let go of my tribal loyalty to England whereas he demonstrated his belief that it is all about the cricket and that has stayed with him throughout his life.

In the prelude to his excellent book, *That Will Be England Done*, Michael Henderson[5] draws a distinction between the cricket fan and the cricket lover. Speaking rather pejoratively he suggests that being a fan implies a form of fanaticism, even tribalism, whereas for the cricket lover the game is invariably more important than winning or losing. In my experience these things are not mutually exclusive. It is more a matter of degree.

As demonstrated earlier by his immediate devotion to Caribbean cricket, Roy would be accurately defined as a cricket lover, but sitting beside him as England struggled towards a famous Ashes victory at Trent Bridge in 2005 was to observe the highs and lows of a dedicated fan.

I am in all things more competitive and also more combative than Roy and would most easily be described as a fan for whom winning or losing, especially against the old enemy, ranks very highly in my priorities. However, as England struggled in that match against the wiles of the great leg-spinner, Shane Warne, I was filled with admiration for the brilliant cricket he was playing as he totally mesmerised the England batsmen. We are both of us fans and lovers of the game, just with a slightly different emphasis.

Soon after our experience at Lord's we both became obsessed with watching Test cricket on television where full coverage was provided by the BBC. In fact, the only time our dad would allow us to stay indoors and watch TV was when a Test match was being broadcast.

There are no doubt many reasons why cricket has become less popular over the years, but I am certain that the removal of the game from terrestrial television has played its part. At 6pm on the day of an international match the parkland behind our house was quiet, but at 6.30pm it was packed with children. A bat and a ball was produced, jumpers were utilised as wickets and the kids from the surrounding streets were out there impersonating their cricketing heroes.

Chapter Seven

Watching the Ashes

AS ANYONE with a passing interest in cricket knows, the Ashes is the name given to any Test series played between England and Australia and the Ashes are held by the team that most recently won the Test series. The term originated in a satirical obituary published in a British newspaper, *The Sporting Times*, immediately after Australia's 1882 victory in a one-off match at the Kennington Oval, their first Test win on English soil. The obituary stated that English cricket had died, and 'the body will be cremated, and the ashes taken to Australia'. The mythical ashes immediately became associated with the 1882/83 series played in Australia shortly afterwards, providing England with an early opportunity to put things right as they saw it. Before the team set sail the English captain Ivo Bligh vowed to 'regain those ashes'.

After England had won two of the three Tests on the tour, a small urn was presented to Bligh. The contents of the urn are reputed to be the ashes of a wooden bail.

From the late 1970s and through the 80s I had a resurgence of watching live Test cricket courtesy of Peter Arnold, former player for Northamptonshire and, during the period in question, chairman of Northamptonshire's cricket committee. As I mentioned in chapter three, he was the father of my good friend, Ewen. I am not sure how, but he seemed able to acquire tickets for us for just about any Test match, irrespective of venue or opposition, including Ashes matches.

I recall watching England beat Pakistan at Lord's in 1978, their victory against India at Edgbaston in 1979 and the draw with the West Indies at Old Trafford in 1980.

Ewen's dad never managed to get us tickets for the Members' Pavilion, that would have been asking too much, but this did not prevent his son seamlessly gaining access. He would casually saunter past the man whose job it was to inspect passes with a wave of the hand and a brisk, 'Good morning!' I would follow in his slipstream trying not to look too guilty. He would then seat himself wherever took his fancy and confidently turn to the member next to him.

'Has Benjamin been in this morning?' he would enquire with the poshest of posh accents.

The recipient of his irresistible bonhomie would invariably pretend he knew the entirely fictitious 'Benjamin' and give some rambling reply. In the unlucky event that someone returned to find Ewen in his seat, he would simply pat 'my dear chap' on the back with some half-baked apology, saying what a duffer he was.

Moving on to the Ashes in 1981, my memory becomes hazy given the number of times that I have watched every match replayed on television. For a long time, I was certain that I was there at Headingley for the famous Ian Botham Test, but a recent conversation with Ewen helped me realise it was the Saturday of the Old Trafford match that we went to. It was when he mentioned Chris Tavaré, the England batsman, that I remembered.

Over the years I have tried to blot out the memory of that Tavaré innings. Watching him bat was a desperate experience at the best of times. Even the wholly objective Wikipedia describes Tavaré's style of play as 'characterised by long periods at the crease and a relatively slow rate of run scoring'. On this particular occasion he clawed his way to 78 in just over seven hours as he defended the bad balls just as resolutely as the good ones. Worse still, Tavaré's approach seemed to be affecting the other players and in the Saturday morning session England scored a miserable 29 runs in 28 overs.

During the lunch interval, Ewen and I looked up at the skies and prayed for rain, but the Manchester weather remained typically cold and damp, but not really wet. When the fifth wicket went down just after lunch the crowd groaned as they realised it was Tavaré who had survived.

But then came redemption! Swinging his bat above his head like a windmill that had lost its moorings, England's stout-hearted hero strode to the wicket. Eighty balls and six sixes later Botham, with Tavaré statuesque at the other end, had reached his century and the Ashes were as good as won.

* * *

Over the next 20 years or so I watched at least one match from each home Ashes series, always hoping in vain to witness another series that could compare to 1981. Ewen went to live and work abroad and my cricket-watching partnership with my brother Roy was re-established. Although England won the series in 1985 followed by victory in Australia two years later, there then followed a serious decline in English fortunes as Australia took over from the West Indies as the dominant force in international cricket.

Australia won every series over a period of 18 years, but in 2005 England, who had not lost a Test match throughout the previous year, had been talking up their own chance of success with their captain, Michael Vaughan, particularly vocal. Vaughan seemed to instil a belief in his team that they could win, that the Aussies could be beaten.

Many regard it as the greatest ever Test series and I would not argue with that. England were hammered in the first Test and won the second by just two runs.

By the time the third Test at Old Trafford came along the whole country had become consumed by the Ashes. As was normal practice at the time, Old Trafford had only issued tickets for the first four days. However, when the fifth day became so crucial with an England victory in sight they announced admission on day five would be through payment at the gate of just £10 and £5 for children. The day's play was due to start at 10.30am, but by 8am chaos surrounded the stadium as the whole of Manchester ground to a halt.

Some people had been waiting all night and queues seemed to be forming everywhere. Estimates of the numbers locked out vary, but it was certainly more than the 19,000 who ended up inside watching the match. In the end the last two Australian batsmen hung on to force a draw when English victory had seemed certain.

Roy and I, as well as my daughter Emily and her husband Andrew, had tickets for every day of the fourth Test at Nottingham's Trent Bridge. After the Old Trafford match had been drawn it was clear that victory in this match by either side would likely prove decisive.

Having batted and bowled well throughout the match England found themselves in a position to make Australia follow on. Despite being a long way behind in the match Australia fought hard. Matthew Hayden and Justin Langer gave their team a 50-run opening stand before Hayden fell to Flintoff, bringing the Australian captain Ricky Ponting to the crease. Ponting was in fine form following his century in the previous game and he reached 50 effortlessly. Then disaster struck. Damien Martyn pushed the ball towards the off side and the two batsmen ran through for a quick single. Gary Pratt, the 12th man and one of the best young fielders available, hurtled across, picked up the ball cleanly and threw it to the striker's end, a direct hit. Ponting was so short of his crease the square leg umpire gave him out without even asking for a TV replay which had become the norm. The England team surrounded Pratt and lifted him off the ground.

Throughout the series England had been deploying the country's best fielders to act as 12th man. Duncan Fletcher, England's head coach, and Vaughan had been searching for every possible advantage as they looked to mastermind a long-sought-after Ashes triumph and this was one of their strategies. This in itself was within the rules, but the hand-picked substitute fielder would routinely replace England's fast bowlers between spells to allow them to get showered and freshen up. The legitimacy of this tactic was somewhat uncertain and had been annoying the Australian hierarchy throughout. In truth this was the sort of hard-nosed strategy that the Australians had been deploying against England for years.

Ponting was furious and, as he marched towards the pavilion, he yelled at the England balcony in anger and frustration, accusing England of cheating and defying the spirit of the game. However, Ponting had not chosen the best moment to complain. Simon Jones, who Gary Pratt had replaced, was in hospital with a serious injury that eventually ended his career. England had truly got under the skin of the mighty Australians.

In the end Australia put on 387, leaving England needing just 129 to win. A doddle, surely? Marcus Trescothick went off like a steam train, doing most of the scoring as 32 runs came in five overs. It was looking like England would win at a canter, when Ponting decided to go to his spinner, not just any spinner, but the great Shane Warne.

Warne stood by the stumps and very slowly and carefully began to move the fielders around. He looked about him as he spun the ball from one hand to the other again and again. He took another look at his field and moved a couple of players back to where they had started. Even then he wasn't quite ready. After a short discussion with his captain, he made one more change to the field. All this time Trescothick had to stand and wait.

In his autobiography, *No Spin*, Shane Warne describes the art of leg spin as 'creating something that is not really there. It is a magic trick, surrounded by mystery, aura and fear.'[2] Warne the magician was busy weaving his spell, setting Trescothick up for the sting that was to come. It was mesmerising and he hadn't even bowled yet!

Warne eventually delivered his first ball. Trescothick pushed forward but couldn't keep it down and Ponting took a low catch at short leg.

Two overs later, he pitched one outside Vaughan's leg stump and as the ball shot past him it clipped the outside edge and went to slip. Our earlier confidence was rapidly disappearing. Strauss then seemed to settle the ship as England passed 50 and our nerves steadied a little but Warne, came around the wicket to the left-handed Strauss. The ball turned sharply and landed in the hands of Michael Clarke at leg slip. Our nerves were now completely frayed, and we watched on with horror as Brett Lee got Ian Bell with a short-pitched delivery. England had been 32/0 and were now reduced to 57 with four wickets down.

We all reacted in different ways. I remained absurdly optimistic whereas Roy was already sure that the Ashes had been lost. Emily was uncharacteristically quiet and

Andy kept leaving his seat in favour of some unknown destination. A young lad behind me carried on a frenzied commentary of events for the benefit of an undefined audience. As the tension increased the pitch of his voice got ever higher.

As Pietersen and Flintoff took England past 100 we settled down again, with me telling the others not to be so stupid.

'We only need 20 odd and we've still got six wickets in hand. Just calm down everyone!'

The words stuck in my throat as Lee, bowling at the speed of light, got Pietersen and shortly after pegged back Flintoff's off stump. Geraint Jones, the wicketkeeper and only recognised batsman left, scratched around for a few overs before deciding to do or die. His nerves shattered and his common sense deserting him, he charged down the wicket and lofted Warne high in the air exactly towards where we were sat. The lad with the frenzied voice whooped for joy, certain it was a six. Below us the boundary fielder waited patiently for the ball to land safely in his hands. 116/7 and surely doomed.

Every minute felt like an hour as the vast and now almost silent crowd sat head in hands in a catatonic state. You could hear a pin drop. Roy looked at the ground and just mumbled words of despair as certain defeat stared him in the eyes.

'Why did we ever think we would beat them? They always find a way.'

Somehow this summed up our collective gloom, our complete absence of hope now laid bare after 18 years of setbacks and failure.

Emily had moved on from biting her fingernails and now had her whole hand in her mouth. To make matters worse for her, proud as she was of her good looks, a Channel 4 cameraman filmed her despondent face and spread it far and wide, across continents as well as into the homes of her many friends.

Her husband Andrew had disappeared again, this time to the otherwise empty toilets. The only person he found there was a cleaning lady taking advantage of the sudden lack of customers. She told him not to be so stupid and to get back to support his team. He walked wordlessly back to his seat like a condemned man where he remained in an unresponsive stupor staring ahead. The voice of the young man behind us had got higher and higher and now virtually disappeared off the scale to the point where it could only be heard by foxes and wolves.

Only two people in Trent Bridge that day believed it could be done and luckily they were the two men at the wicket.

Matthew Hoggard, a red-faced rural Yorkshireman, hardly knew which end of the bat to hold, but apparently he came to the wicket and told Ashley Giles, 'Come on, Gilo, let's get this done.'

Ashley Giles later revealed that he told Hoggard that Brett Lee was reverse-swinging the ball at 95mph. 'I thought he ought to know,' he said.

Each ball was an event and slowly, very slowly England edged forward until Hoggard, his body and mind apparently taken over by the spirit of some great Yorkshire batsman of the past, drove sweetly through the covers for four. The place erupted, not with joy, but sheer relief. Soon after Giles hit the winning shot, completing the second run with his bat held aloft. Trent Bridge exploded and the country rejoiced.

Five hours and several pints later the adrenalin was still pumping through our veins and we were struggling to control our emotions. The four of us were trying to decide where to eat and Roy and I, who even as kids rarely argued and never fell out, were at each other's throats trying to decide between a Chinese restaurant and going to the chippy! With the matter unresolved we simply stayed at the pub and, without food to mop up the beer, got hopelessly pissed.

As is traditional, the final Test was to be held at the Oval with England needing only a draw to claim the Ashes. Immediately after the fourth Test at Trent Bridge my confidence was sky high and I really felt that the Ashes were almost in the bag. However, as the fifth Test approached my normal state of anxiety returned. Of course, a win for Australia would mean the series was tied and they would retain the urn. Talking to Roy on the phone during the build-up only dampened my optimism further. I recalled his words on the final day at Trent Bridge.

'Why did we ever think we would beat them? They always find a way.'

Although the match ebbed and flowed, the constant intervention of the weather appeared to ensure the draw we needed would be achieved.

I had watched quite a lot of the match on the TV, but on the final day this was not possible. I was working for the children's charity, Barnardo's, at the time and on that very day our management team were at a hotel on a team building exercise. As assistant director I obviously had a big part to play in proceedings. Luckily for me two members of the hotel staff were cricket enthusiasts, and they had the match running on the lounge bar TV all day. I called in at the bar during the morning break to check the score and watch for ten minutes. A draw was looking likely with England on their second innings at 65/1, 71 runs ahead. They just needed to bat for most of the day to ensure that Australia did not have any realistic target to chase in their second innings. So far everything was going to plan. However, I went back to the bar at lunchtime to find England had been reduced to 127/5, a lead of just 133.

I returned to the team building event in a state of real anxiety and found it hard to concentrate. I think my colleagues were wondering what was going on as I took a ridiculous number of toilet breaks and on several occasions left the room on the spurious grounds that I needed something from the car. At about 2.45pm one of the waiters indicated with a raise of the eyebrows that things were unravelling. England had now lost their seventh wicket. I could pretend no longer. I announced that I would have to leave the event and go and watch the cricket. Before my colleagues could react I was gone, leaving them open-mouthed.

With my two new friends I watched Kevin Pietersen pull things around with a fine century. With my professional reputation in tatters the team building day progressed without me while I sat in the hotel bar and, after an 18-year wait, finally witnessed England regain the Ashes.

Roy's daughter Rebecca has an Australian friend who lives near to Roy and for the whole Test series he had been insisting in a most bullish manner that England would be beaten in the end. As soon as the game was over Roy had a few beers and headed for the Australian's house. He knocked smartly on the door and, receiving no reply, began to call the guy's name from the garden.

'Come on out! You've been beaten. Come and face the music!'

With silence maintained from within his voice got louder, his mood more obdurate and his tone more belligerent. He paced up and down having little care for the state of the man's garden as he trampled on asters, chrysanthemums and dahlias, all renowned for their late blooming. Five days later, having already suffered from his country losing the Ashes, the poor man returned from holiday to find his garden had been trashed!

* * *

In 2015 England approached the fourth Test, again at Trent Bridge, slightly more secure than in 2005, already 2-1 up in the series. However, their senior bowler, Jimmy Anderson, was unavailable through injury and media speculation centred on whether Stuart Broad could step up to lead the attack.

Not for the first time, with Anderson absent, Broad did something sensational. It was a day to pity anyone who stopped on their way to Trent Bridge to pick up a paper or buy some sandwiches for their lunch. Even if they only missed the first over the pleasure of seeing the wickets of Chris Rogers and Steve Smith would have been denied them. If, like four guys occupying the seats next to me, they arrived an hour late they would already have missed the fastest five-wicket haul (19 balls) in the history of Test cricket.

Roy and I had only been able to acquire two seats that set us a couple of rows apart in the William Clarke Stand so all we could do was stare at each other as the carnage took place before our eyes. The sight of Broad running in to bowl as six slips crouched in anticipation of yet another wicket was a joy to witness. Broad bowled unchanged, taking eight wickets for just 15 runs, and 20 minutes before lunch on the first day Australia were all out for 60. Only two players reached double figures. As so often before Broad had saved his best for his home ground.

My daughter Emily was on holiday in Cornwall and she and the family had spent the day on the beach. They got back to the car and Andy put the radio on just as England left the field at the end of day one.

Since 2005 there had been a special Ashes bond between the four of us and they were anxious to know that we had enjoyed the day.

Immediately she heard the England score she was on the phone.

'That's not a bad day, dad, 274/4 at the close. Who got the runs?'

As I told her about Root's century it dawned on me that she had no idea what had happened beforehand. She did not realise that Australia had already batted. As I described the events of the morning no reaction came back. She was in a complete state of shock and disbelief.

* * *

I said earlier that if you watch as much international cricket as Roy and I then you will be there for many of the memorable moments. However, it does not always work that way. There have been at least two occasions that I can recall where we have very much watched the wrong part of an Ashes match.

In July 2009 Roy and I together with my youngest daughter Lucy and her boyfriend (now husband) Tom gathered for the first Ashes Test and the first ever Test to be held in Wales. We had a great campsite on the banks of the River Taff with a short and picturesque walk to the ground. All was set fair. England batted first and at a scoring rate above four an over got to 435 before lunch on the second day. This seemed like a good score until Australia countered with 674 including four centuries and declared leaving England needing 239 just to make Australia bat again.

We were there throughout the first four days and tickets were readily available for day five, during which England needed to survive from a starting point of 20/2. Lucy and Tom were forced to return due to work commitments whereas Roy and I could choose whether to attend the last day or not.

Bearing in mind we had two years earlier travelled to Australia for a 5-0 mauling we were not ultra-keen to hang about for another thrashing. However, engaging my normal optimism in the face of looming disaster, I persuaded Roy to hang about at the campsite until the direction of the game became clear. Woefully, at lunch England were 70/5 and surely doomed. We packed up our things and left in opposite directions to drive home.

The rest is history. Paul Collingwood's gritty innings lasted 245 balls. Five hours and 43 minutes he was at the crease, but with still about 12 overs to go he was out, bringing together the last-wicket pair of Jimmy Anderson and Monty Panesar, probably the worst batsman in Test cricket. Unlikely saviours indeed. I got home just in time to witness their moment of triumph as they held out against all odds to force a draw. It was an uncharacteristic lack of loyalty from Roy and me for which we paid heavily.

The other occasion was much more recent, in the Ashes summer of 2019. Since becoming members of Notts County Cricket Club getting tickets for Test matches had become considerably easier, but in 2019 we were taken by surprise when we realised none of the Tests were scheduled to take place at Trent Bridge. After a lot of effort, we managed to acquire tickets for days one and two at Yorkshire's famous ground, Headingley.

I had brought my caravan and we were already set up the afternoon prior to the match on a beautiful campsite at Wharfedale. The nearby village of Bramhope offered a very friendly pub with good food and excellent ale, a fish and chip shop and a bakery selling sandwiches and rolls. There was a bus service directly to the ground. What more could two cricket fans who loved their ale want?

Whenever we use buses Roy always has something to say about the validity of my bus pass. I live in Wales and, rather annoyingly, it is not valid in other UK nations including England. So much for the *United* Kingdom.

When we got on the bus on the first day Roy was looking forward to my pass being rejected, knowing that I would doggedly present it. He placed his pass in front of the scanner and was rewarded with a positive ringing sound. When it came to my turn the machine made the sort of hooting noise that often accompanies wrong answers on game shows. Undeterred, I immediately started arguing with the driver. As is usually my experience he just gave in.

'Just go and sit down, mate,' he sighed wearily.

With a beaming smile from me and a scowl from Roy we found a seat.

On day two we got on board expecting the same scene to be played out. Roy took his bus pass from his wallet as I, bringing up the rear, held mine aloft with an air of defiance.

'Sorry, mate, that's not valid!' the driver said immediately.

Roy turned back to me with a smile of triumph spreading across his face. 'See, at least this guy knows the rules. You heard the man. It's not valid.'

The driver tapped him on the shoulder and Roy turned to face him with the knowing look of a man who likes to play by the rules.

'No, mate, I mean yours isn't valid. It's not 9.30 yet. Two returns to the ground, is it?'

Roy nodded feebly.

'That'll be seven quid mate!'

I was still laughing when we got to the ground where I sang 'Jerusalem' with even more pride than usual.

To get back to the cricket, a weather-restricted first day had ended at 7.30pm with Australia 179 all out, a brilliant start for England. That evening Roy and I sat in the Fox and Hounds with our pints in front of us in a mellow mood. Jofra Archer had truly come of age as a Test match bowler with six wickets and we had another full day of cricket ahead of us during which England would no doubt take the upper hand in the match. What could possibly go wrong?

The following morning we were up bright and early. After the bus pass incident we went into the ground, bought a coffee and a bun and waited for the action to begin.

England were six wickets down at lunch and half an hour later they were all out for 67! Only one player managed double figures. This was a true debacle, and one that could have reverberated for a long time to come.

That evening our mood sitting in the Fox and Hounds was considerably more sombre. In fact we were angry at the abject surrender we had witnessed. We love watching international cricket and can usually forgive our team almost anything, but on this occasion we were ready to tear them down.

We were sick of the 'Team England' approach always wanting to 'learn going forward'. As far as we were concerned at that moment it was time to bring an end to the 'Root Project' and start looking for a new captain. We even talked of appointing the one-day captain, Eoin Morgan, worth his place as a captain and leader even if he was yet to prove his credentials as a Test batsman. We just wanted to see some good old-fashioned fight and did not believe it would happen under Root.

The following morning we headed home, rather as we had in July 2009 at Cardiff, with no real belief that England could save the match let alone win it. It was a good job that we had been staying in a stunning location and had enjoyed our time in the Yorkshire countryside. Had it not been for this we would have gone home feeling pretty depressed.

Australia's second innings was fairly poor with only the new sensation, Marnus Labuschagne, scoring any runs. By the time I got home Australia were all out for just 246, but due to our first innings debacle had still managed to set England a target of 359 which history told us was virtually impossible. However, England started their second innings just about well enough at the end of day four for me to settle myself in front of the telly the following morning with just a glimmer of belief.

On the Sunday morning Root was out almost immediately and when Bairstow followed and Buttler soon after I wandered out to see what needed doing in the garden.

I am a keen gardener, growing all my own vegetables as well as growing bedding plants, mainly for hanging baskets. I have a number of raised beds as well as a huge polytunnel. August is a nice month for growers as there are usually peas, french beans, courgettes and some varieties of potatoes to be harvested as well as cucumbers and if you are lucky some cherry tomatoes.

As I had been away for a few days at the cricket there was quite a lot to do and as is often the case I soon lost myself in the various tasks. It was therefore several hours before I returned to the living room to catch up on the cricket. I put the TV on just as Ben Stokes hit a six to take England past 300. I was about to celebrate when I saw the wickets column and realised that his partner was the last man Jack Leach and England still needed more than 50 runs for victory.

Watching Leach studiously polishing his glasses between overs I was reminded of the legendary commentator, John Arlott, describing another unlikely hero from yesteryear, the bespectacled David Steele, as 'like a bank clerk going to war'.

From that moment on I, along with cricket fans all over the world, sat glued to the television as Stokes made the impossible happen and Nasser Hussain on commentary almost had a seizure. Many cricket pundits regard this innings as even topping Botham at Headingley in 1981. It was hard to take that Roy and I had been there, but at the wrong end of the match. Mind you, I'm not sure our hearts would have stood it.

Chapter Eight

The Burger Moment and Other Cricketing Anecdotes

ROY AND I have been members of Nottinghamshire County Cricket Club for some time, but long before we officially signed up we had already been watching Test cricket for many years. Trent Bridge in Nottingham is without doubt our favourite ground. The experience of watching a Test match there is markedly different from watching at the other northern grounds that we frequent.

This is largely down to the friendliness of the stewards whose *raison d'etre* seems to be to enhance your enjoyment. The stewards at some other Test grounds seem to be intent on policing anti-social behaviour which, to their apparent disappointment, rarely arises. The stewards at Trent Bridge face the cricket whereas at other locations they face the crowd. For Roy and me that says it all.

The only other ground where we have experienced stewards with a similar approach was at the SWALEC Stadium in Cardiff where we watched the first Ashes Test match in 2009 that I discussed in chapter seven. I hope and trust their friendly approach has been sustained.

All of the Test match grounds have been renovated in recent years, but only Trent Bridge has maintained its essential spirit. Old Trafford today looks as if two enormous red juggernauts have collided with the cricket ground and nobody has had the wherewithal to remove them. Trent Bridge, on the other hand, has been updated incrementally, improving facilities without any loss to the character and charm of the place. Most importantly the old pavilion is unchanged. So as we sit there watching 21st century matches, our memories of watching great players of the past move up and down those steps are unsullied.

Given the amount of Test matches we go to it is not surprising that we often find ourselves in the right place at the right time just as something extraordinary is happening. This was certainly the case at Trent Bridge in 2011 where England were playing India in the second Test.

Both Roy and I are avid observers of other spectators and could not help paying particular attention to two young friends sitting just in front of us. One was a rather fleshy-faced lad with a pimply complexion and a mouth that never seemed to be still even when he was neither eating nor speaking. Although how I made this observation I am not sure as he seemed to be doing one or the other most of the time. To be fair though, he did know his cricket. His friend by contrast knew absolutely nothing about the game and so his fleshy-lipped pal was keeping him comprehensively informed as the game progressed.

The tourists were in total control of the match, already leading by 46 on 267/4, when our pimply pal announced he was going for a pee and to fetch himself a burger. I resisted the temptation to tell him to wash his hands between the two activities. Off he went, giving himself and his friend a well-earned rest from each other.

Almost as soon as he had disappeared behind the stands Nottingham's own Stuart Broad dismissed Yuvraj Singh for 62 to break his partnership of 128 with centurion Rahul Dravid.

Then in his next over Broad had MS Dhoni caught in the slips, Harbhajan Singh trapped leg before wicket and Praveen Kumar clean bowled in successive balls. The crowd at his home ground went crazy, shouting and whooping with joy. It was his first hat-trick for England, but by no means his last.

Presumably somewhere in the bowels of the ground the sound of celebration must have been heard by our young friend, but he returned to his seat, chomping at his burger, apparently oblivious to what had happened in his absence. He made himself comfortable and looked up at the scoreboard no doubt with the intention of taking up his narrative.

Slowly a bemused look spread across his pock-marked face. He looked pleadingly at his pal who was, alas, unable to help. Eventually his friend made some attempt to recall the details of what he had witnessed.

'I'm not sure why, but lots of Indian players seemed to be coming and going,' he proffered.

I could feel the cogs in his brain turning as he tried to make sense of it all. Yuvraj Singh was certainly gone, but how could the numbers in the wicket column have gone from four to eight in less than ten minutes?

Roy tapped him on the shoulder wanting, as with a fatally wounded animal, to put him out of his misery.

'Broad got Yuvraj Singh just after you got up and then completed a hat-trick in the next over,' he explained.

The look in the young man's eyes betrayed a hideous self-pity as he stared down at his burger with loathing. I don't recall hearing him speak again for the rest of the day.

Fifteen minutes later he looked on in a self-induced trance as Broad removed last man Ishant Sharma to wrap up the India innings and complete a 16-ball spell of five wickets for no runs. Somehow he would have to explain to his mates back home that he was there on the day that Stuart Broad single-handedly turned the match, but he had missed it all in one badly timed burger moment.

It was a remarkable period of play that left Broad's many admirers grasping for superlatives to describe his performance. Incredibly he had earlier in the match engineered England's first comeback, scoring a rapid 64 to rescue his team from 124/8 to 221 all out in their first innings.

England went on to win the match by a considerable margin and fittingly it was Broad who finished the game off with a yorker into the base of Sri Sreesanth's middle stump.

We thought at the time that this was to be Broad's greatest match, but as described earlier just a few seasons on he was to reach even greater heights by taking eight wickets in an Ashes match, again at Trent Bridge.

Several years later Roy and I spotted the burger boy watching an England match at Old Trafford. He was only a few rows in front of us. To the people around him he was just another quiet fan supporting his team in his own undemonstrative way, but we knew better. His natural exuberance and *joie de vivre* had long since departed. The burger incident had left him a broken man.

* * *

As was the case with the burger moment there are some matches that stay in the memory for reasons only loosely connected with the cricket. Often the memories stick when things don't go exactly to plan.

Just such an occasion was in 1998 at Headingley, Leeds where England were playing South Africa. It was the final Test and with the series 1-1 it was also the decider. Emily, her partner Andy and I had tickets for the third day, a Saturday, and with honours even in a low-scoring match we were very much looking forward to the action.

On the previous day I had been doing some work outside and had turned my ankle. It hurt for about ten minutes and was then fine. I gave the matter no further thought. On Saturday morning the alarm went off at six, giving us plenty of time to get from North Wales to Leeds. I swung my legs out of bed, tried to stand up and landed in a heap on the floor. I had sprained my ankle and could not walk.

Still on the floor, I grabbed the bedside phone and rang Emily. She sounded groggy, but I was not surprised by this. We were due to leave at 7.30am so she would have set her alarm for about 7.20!

'I can't go. My ankle is the size of a pumpkin and I can't walk. It's probably broken,' I added for maximum impact.

'Course it isn't broken. Is your foot still pointing forward?'

I had to admit it was.

'Well it's not broken then!'

She was quite dogmatic about it, but quite how 'A' levels in English and fine art qualified her to make such a firm telephone diagnosis, I wasn't sure.

As a child Emily had been an able and fearsome sportswoman and in her short life had broken every limb that could be broken.

'I've got some crutches here. We're going! Andrew's been looking forward to it.'

Andrew, who she later married, was the new love in Emily's life and pleasing him easily outweighed the prospect of her father being crippled for life. Also, I was the only one with a car.

Fifteen minutes later she appeared in the kitchen with two crutches under her arm. Immediately she demonstrated how easy they were to use by flashing around our kitchen on one leg at a ferocious pace. I knew I was done. Tentatively I took the crutches from her and tried them out. As long as I kept my injured leg off the ground I could get about, albeit rather slowly.

'See, you're fine. By the time we get to Leeds you'll be an expert,' she maintained, although how I was to practise whilst sitting in the back of the car for three hours escaped me.

I tried to enlist my wife's support, but other than to register her disappointment that nobody had brought her a cup of tea, she did not seem particularly interested. Certainly, she had no intention of taking sides.

Shortly before ten and still with an hour to spare before the game we arrived outside the ground. Emily and Andy deposited me on a street corner and went off to find somewhere to park. By the time they returned the effort involved in standing for 20 minutes on one leg was taking its toll and I was glad when we finally went into the ground and found our seats.

The match was going alright. Although Michael Atherton had lost his wicket almost as soon as we arrived, Nasser Hussain and Mark Butcher were starting to build a partnership. Andy had bought everyone a pint and glasses were now empty. It was my round.

I stood up and settled on my crutches.

'Bitter is it, Andy?' Emily had decided to have a few drinks in the morning and then no more as she was driving. I knew she would want cider. There was no need to ask.

'Andy will go, dad. You don't want to be hobbling all the way to the bar.'

Andy was immediately on his feet, but my stubborn independent streak caused me to insist.

'No, it's my round. Anyway, I'm pretty good on these now.'

Emily started to object, but quickly saw it was futile. I set off in the direction of the bar, causing havoc as everyone sitting in our row had to virtually leave their seat for me to get out.

I arrived at the bar in good order and with as much bonhomie as I could muster ordered the drinks. The girl behind the bar set the three glasses on the counter and looked at me. Simultaneously it dawned on us both that I had no means of carrying them!

'Oh shit,' I murmured as a smile broke out on the girl's face.

Immediately she lifted the hatch, came round to the customers' side and picked up the glasses.

'I'll follow you,' she said.

I felt completely stupid but was extremely grateful for her offer. Five minutes later, I was back at base and poor Andy found himself trying to explain why he had allowed a man on crutches to fetch the drinks. Emily made no such effort. Instead she just looked at me and shook her head.

After that I was allowed toilet breaks at lunch and tea but was otherwise ordered to stay in my seat. On the pitch things went well with England reaching 206 for the loss of four wickets. Despite everything we had spent an enjoyable day.

Outside the ground we went through the morning routine in reverse, that is I waited on the street by the ground while Emily and Andy went to fetch the car. Remembering the discomfort of standing waiting for them in the morning, I started searching for somewhere to sit. There was no obvious place, but eventually I spotted a stone wall surrounding someone's garden. I hopped over to it, but when I stood by it I saw it was higher than I had realised. Leaving the crutches on the ground, I backed towards the wall and placed my hands on top. Pushing with my hands and my good leg I tried to get on to the wall, but with just one leg I could not get the elevation I needed.

A new plan was required. I picked up the crutches and backed against the wall again. I crouched down and then using the crutches and my uninjured leg I gave an almighty heave upwards, reminiscent of the Fosbury flop used in modern high jump.

It was spectacularly successful and clearing the wall I landed on my bum in a large, thankfully forgiving hydrangea bush. My legs and crutches were the only things visible from the street. This all occurred while 15,000 people were leaving the ground so I had a decent audience. Unable to right myself, I laid there helpless while all those watching fell about laughing. Eventually the laughter was followed by spontaneous applause, and this was the scene to which my daughter and future son-in-law returned. Later Emily confided that they had seriously considered walking away.

* * *

Over the next few years I watched several matches together with Emily and Andy, often with Roy as well, but sometimes just the three of us. A number of years after the crutches incident I was again with Emily and Andy when a different disaster overtook us.

In 2008 their first child Finlay was born, but both parents were determined to continue to watch cricket whenever they could. Early in the 2010 season I idly announced that I was considering going to Trent Bridge to watch one or two days of Nottinghamshire's game against Durham starting on 10 May. Durham had won the County Championship in 2008 and again in 2009. For the forthcoming season the only serious contenders were Nottinghamshire. It had the makings of an excellent match.

Emily and her family now lived in a small village just a few miles from us. All of us were really down following Labour's disastrous showing at the General Election held on 6 May 2010. At least one of us had been out canvassing every day for the last four weeks so it was doubly disappointing. It was looking likely that the Liberal Democrats would join the Tories to form a coalition and we were in need of some fun to take our mind off politics so it was no surprise when Emily and Andy announced that they would join me at Trent Bridge.

Fin was now 18 months old and already tottering around. However, as hard as Emily and Andy had worked on it, he was not yet an interested cricket fan! The plan was to take him into the ground and just see how he fared. If it proved too difficult they would simply take it in turns to look after him.

We decided to take the caravan down on the evening of the second day with a view to watching day three and, if the game justified it, day four.

We arrived at about four in the afternoon, set up the caravan and awning and thought about finding a pub serving food. We did eventually find somewhere with a beer garden, had a couple of pints and ordered our dinner. All three of us are vegetarians so the meals we ordered would not have been very exotic, although I do recall that Emily had a vegetable chilli.

Fin was really good and was in bed and fast asleep by nine. We were not far behind him and turned in at about ten. At around two in the morning Emily was feeling sick and went off to the campsite loo. I thought no more of it until I woke up just before six to be told she was really unwell. An hour later I had to accompany her to the loo as she felt she may not make it. Andy was busy with Finlay.

I waited for her outside the ladies' toilet block and after hearing nothing from her for about ten minutes she shouted out to me.

'Dad, I can't feel my legs!'

'What do you mean, you can't feel them?'

She started to cry. 'They're sort of paralysed. I can't get up.'

My daughter Emily had been a drama queen all her life with a healthy tendency to exaggerate things, but over her lifetime I had learned to differentiate between froth and real disasters. This came into the second category. As far as I could tell there was nobody else in the toilet block. I looked around and satisfied myself that no one was approaching. I was just about to enter the building when Emily appeared in the doorway clutching the wall.

She looked dreadful. Her face was as white as a sheet and her mouth seemed distorted in some way. Her eyes were filled with tears. Her knees were buckling beneath her and she looked on the verge of passing out.

'I think I've been poisoned,' she said, looking really alarmed.

Somehow I got her back to the caravan and we quickly decided she needed to get to hospital. Andy, who had not until this moment realised how bad things were, got on his phone and located the local A&E. Within five minutes he and Emily were on their way in my car to the Queen's Medical Centre, part of Nottingham University Hospitals. I stayed behind to look after Finlay, a task I was more than used to as he spent three days a week with us.

While Emily and Andy were gone, besides trying to keep Fin entertained, I attempted to keep up to date with the match that we had intended to watch. Finally, I tuned in to BBC Nottingham on the car radio, who gave half-hourly updates. By the end of the previous evening Notts had reached 191/3 in reply to Durham's first innings score of 218. On the day in question they sped along and thanks to rapid centuries from Ally Brown and Chris Read they were able to declare on 559/8 having achieved this mammoth score in just 118 overs. As a result they still had 32 overs to bowl at Durham in which time they took four wickets.

Emily and Andy finally returned at about 6.30pm just as the players were leaving the field. They had arrived at A&E where Emily was able to bypass the normal lengthy waiting time by fainting before she had even sat down. Apparently she awoke on a hospital trolley with a drip in her arm on the way to a ward. She had some form of bacterial food poisoning, possibly salmonella. Salmonella is one of the most common types of food poisoning that usually causes stomach cramps and diarrhoea that lasts four to seven days. However, the symptoms can be more serious for some people and Emily seemed to fall into this category.

The hospital had wanted to admit her, but she was intent on going home so we hitched up the caravan and prepared to leave. Emily was still so unwell she and Andy did toy with the idea of her lying in bed in the caravan for the journey home. However, I vetoed this idea, not believing it to be safe. I also thought we should have her in the car so we could monitor her condition while we travelled. In the end she slumped in the back of the Land Rover alongside Finlay, who sat in his raised seat like a little prince.

I think I drove her mad on the way home by continually asking how she was. Eventually she lost her cool with me.

'I feel bloody awful so stop asking. Just get me home.'

So I stopped asking and got her home, although it was nearly ten at night when we finally arrived. She staggered into the house and went straight to bed.

The following morning I rang Andy to be told Emily was still in bed. She felt really weak, but at least the worst of the symptoms seemed to have passed.

At about 11.30am I caught up with the cricket and learned that Durham had already lost another two wickets. I was sure the game would be over in the next hour or so and I did not look to see what the score was until much later in the afternoon. Durham did go down to a heavy defeat by an innings and 62 runs, but not before a young man of just 18 had scored 106 off 126 balls with 16 fours and three sixes. His previous best county score was 41. Ben Stokes had arrived!

Chapter Nine

In No Particular Order

ON THE afternoon of Saturday, 8 August 1992 my friend Ewen and I were in his car heading down the M6 to London. We had tickets for the following day to see England play Pakistan, as always courtesy of Ewen's dad. The plan was to stay overnight with some friends and then get to the Kennington Oval bright and early for the fourth day.

This was the fifth and final Test and the series was on a knife-edge at 1-1. This match had not been going well since England won the toss and batted. They scored only 207, totally conceding the advantage to Pakistan who made 380 in reply. We chatted for a while about the prospects for the day's play and eventually turned the car radio on with England barely an hour into their second innings. The score stood at 47/1 with Graham Gooch and a very young Michael Atherton appearing solid, or so we thought. The veteran together with the young pretender who, less than a year later, would succeed Gooch as captain.

Then the first blow fell. Waqar Younis got the ball to move away, took the edge of Atherton's bat and he was duly caught behind the stumps, 47/2. Our over-optimistic ramblings ceased for the moment as we each did calculations in our head, plotting England's route out of the mire. We were just coming up for air, our calculations complete when Waqar struck again. This time it was Gooch. In my mind's eye I could see him, a picture of dejection as he left the field of play in his characteristic manner, slouched forward, his head down, dragging his bat behind him.

Ewen must have had a similar image in his head.

'We're doomed!' he exclaimed.

Such was the frailty of England's batting at the time the sight of Gooch getting out often elicited this kind of response. 55/3.

Momentarily we rallied as Robin Smith was joined by David Gower, surely the most stylish batsman England had ever produced. Waqar again, wicket again, Gower was gone, clean bowled. 59/4.

We were now somewhere near Birmingham, about halfway through our journey. Should we go on or cut our losses and go home? Feeling genuinely undecided, we stopped for coffee.

'I'll tell you what,' Ewen began once we had found a seat, 'We'll have this coffee and if no more wickets have fallen we'll go on. If we get back to the car and someone's got out, I'm for turning back.'

I agreed, but it soon became evident that Ewen actually wanted to go home. I base this on the fact that he took ages over his coffee, presumably to give Pakistan the chance to bag another. By the time we got back to the car, almost ten more overs had been bowled. Brian Johnston was on commentary and could be relied upon to give the score at regular intervals. '92/4,' he informed us.

With a resigned smile Ewen put his Volkswagen into gear and headed for London. Three minutes later the fifth wicket fell. He looked at me questioningly.

'A deal's a deal,' I told him and so on we went.

When the close of play arrived it was at first like a merciful release, but soon we were engaged in calculations again.

'We're only 30 odd behind now,' said Ewen, his optimistic juices back in full flow. 'Robin Smith's playing well. If someone can stay with him we could still get 150 ahead and then anything's possible.'

Cricket fans of a certain vintage will know that the phrase 'If someone can stay with him' was at that time as absurdly hopeful as it was implausible. My brother is prone to misquote Jack Nicklaus who, according to Roy, described an under-achieving Canadian golfer as having 'a million-dollar swing and a ten-cent head'. The true quote is 'a ten-cent putter'. However, I liked Roy's version more and it describes England's lower-middle order in the 1990s perfectly. There were some highly talented players who were unfortunately a little light on judgement.

Given we were staying with some of Ewen's old university friends, the idea that we would arrive at the Oval 'bright and early' was somewhat fanciful. We arrived at the ground on time, but certainly not 'bright'. However, we were ready. 'C'mon, England!'

On that morning Robin Smith played beautifully and a century seemed on the cards. Alongside him Chris Lewis played sensibly, leaving most of the striking to his in-form partner. Then suddenly without warning he decided he would go after the spinner, Mushtaq Ahmed, and was stumped.

England were 153/6 and ten overs later were all out, leaving Pakistan needing just two to win. They faced one ball, hit it for four and took the match and the series, while Ewen and I wondered what to do with the rest of the day. The pub beckoned and we duly obliged.

* * *

In June 2006 Roy and I were in Nottingham watching England play Sri Lanka in the third Test. At the end of the second day (Saturday) a low-scoring match was finely balanced. Sri Lanka had posted 231 in their first innings and England had almost reached parity scoring 229. At close Sri Lanka were 45/1 in their second innings. For some reason we had tickets for Monday, but not for the Sunday so we decided to seek out a local match to entertain us for the day. On Sunday morning we bought ourselves a local paper and scanned the sports section for any Sunday afternoon matches. Eventually we found a match to be played at an old miners' cricket club about 40 minutes away. This would do very nicely.

In the event it took us some time to find the old colliery ground and even when we were quite close nobody seemed able to give us directions.

When the coal industry was nationalised in 1947, there were 49 collieries in Nottinghamshire, but by 2006 there were just two. It is amazing how quickly the industrial landscape of an area can change and with it the cultural landscape and the demography. However, none of this prepared us for the fact that nobody seemed to know where the ground was and even less so for the discovery that the whole of the home team were of Asian heritage.

When we did finally arrive the game was already underway and the home team were fielding. Certain things became clear very quickly. Firstly, the standard of bowling and fielding from the home team was very high. Secondly, the majority of the team were below 30 and very fit, but they were captained by a portly gentleman in his late 40s or early 50s. The young members of the team seemed to have little respect for their captain, which I found surprising as respect for your elders is deeply embedded in many Asian cultures. It seemed that getting them to move in the field to where he wanted them was akin to herding cats.

In just a few seconds all that changed. One of the batsmen, who was just starting to find the middle of the bat, pulled the ball to midwicket. The ball was travelling like a meteor, remaining just three feet off the ground as it sped towards the boundary. Suddenly the captain moved to his left and the ball whistled into his ample midriff. As he slumped to the ground all the air was forced from his body, causing the ball to be expelled from the folds of his stomach, luckily into his waiting hands. As he lay there in a winded heap he held the ball aloft in triumph. It was an extraordinary catch. The whole team mobbed him as he grinned like a Cheshire cat. In an instant his authority was restored.

Meanwhile, back at Trent Bridge Sri Lanka won the Test by 134 runs.

* * *

Before settling on a husband, my youngest daughter Lucy had an eclectic taste in boyfriends. The one I liked the most was a young guitar player called Mark who sold socks and underwear at the local market. He was just dead straightforward, but somehow did not suit her and eventually he was dropped. When the end came for each of them she could be sudden and brutal. I remember when she was living and working in Germany her boyfriend of the time flew over to see her. She met him at the airport and told him it was over. He then spent a miserable week alone in a hostel in Frankfurt waiting for his return flight.

In July 2001 I had four tickets for the fourth day of the first Test against Australia. The match was at Edgbaston, Birmingham. Roy was coming from Norfolk and Emily and new husband Andy were coming from London. The plan was that we would all meet at the ground but at the last minute Roy couldn't make it.

Lucy and her current boyfriend, an Australian known as AJ, were staying at ours at the time. AJ was a big cricket fan, but in all other respects not particularly loveable. However, he had just helped me fit some new windows at our house so the decent thing was to offer him the spare ticket which I duly did and soon we were on the train heading for Birmingham.

Meeting Emily at the ground with AJ in tow was not the best start to the day. She really didn't like him. Firstly, the guitar-playing Mark was a friend of hers and she had never understood why Lucy had dumped him. Secondly, she was Lucy's elder sister and no one was good enough for her, but mainly she thought AJ was a self-centred surfer bum and she was probably right.

Anyway, we got over that hiccup and settled down to watch the game. As was usual in those days England were already up against it. They had only made 294 in their first innings, despite an unlikely hundred-run partnership for the last wicket, and Australia had replied with 576.

Now in their second innings, England started the day on 48/1 still 234 behind! At first things looked promising and 20 overs into the day they had progressed to 142/2, although the England captain, Nasser Hussain, had retired hurt following a blow to the hand and it was not known if he would bat again. However, their good progress did not last and just six overs after lunch England were all out, losing the match by an innings and 118 runs.

So here we were in Birmingham in the early afternoon with a gloating Aussie in our midst. Seeing Emily was a rare treat for me and nobody was in the mood to head home after just two and a half hours of cricket so we found a pub to our liking and relaxed. It was a long time since we had seen England win a cricket match and so it was not hard to overcome our disappointment even with AJ chirping in our ear.

Three hours later we had all had more than enough beer so we walked to the train station and went our separate ways. By this time AJ had told me innumerable times that Australia were unbeatable, something I already believed somewhere deep down, but I was getting sick of having it said to me again and again. He was drunk and only 22 or 23 so I tried to make allowances. Nevertheless, I was glad when he fell asleep. Soon enough he was virtually comatose. I noted with interest that our train which we were due to leave at Chester was heading for Glasgow. There was no way he was going to wake up of his own accord and I must admit I was tempted.

It took another year before Lucy tired of him and when the end came it was swift and unsentimental, the verdict delivered in a 60-second phone call! I often wonder if her husband Tom thinks about her penchant for sudden endings. They have been together for ten years so I guess he thinks the danger has passed. I would only say that I have been with her mother for 50 years and I still don't feel secure.

Chapter Ten

Pakistan Spot Fixing Scandal

LIKE MOST sports fans I have a deep-seated hatred of cheating. I hated it when I played sport and equally as a spectator. As a player I could never understand how people who had cheated could get any pleasure from winning. For me it would have completely devalued it.

For many years I played football with a guy who was ultra-competitive, but during the match never knew what the score was. For him playing to the best of his ability, contributing everything he could to the team cause was what competitive sport was all about. He liked to win but had no difficulty with losing. I never managed to emulate that, but I did understand that if there was a winner, by definition, there was a loser.

In terms of tolerance of cheating I have a fairly low threshold. I dislike footballers that dive and cricketers who remain at the crease when they know they are out, although in international cricket the introduction of third umpire reviews has complicated that position.

On Saturday, 28 August 2010 Roy and I had tickets for the third day of the Lord's Test against Pakistan. It was a rare treat for us to get tickets for a Saturday at the 'home of cricket' and we were full of expectation for a great day out. After a very shaky start England had recovered on day two thanks to a so far unbroken partnership in excess of 200 between Jonathan Trott and his unlikely partner, Stuart Broad.

Roy and I watched in awe as they continued to batter the Pakistani bowling attack, eventually sharing a world record-breaking partnership of 332. Pakistan replied with a dismal first innings total of 74 and then proceeded to lose four second innings wickets following on.

It had been a breathtaking day's cricket and we were both disappointed to be heading home without the opportunity of talking through the day's proceedings over a pint or two.

Roy's journey home to Norfolk was shorter than mine and when I did eventually get back to North Wales there was a telephone message telling me to ring him as soon as I got home whatever the time. Slightly alarmed by the message, I rang him at about 11.30pm.

I could never have guessed what he wanted to tell me. I stood motionless as he related the spot-fixing story of no-balls to order involving Salman Butt, Mohammad Asif and Mohammad Amir, the latter having etched his name on the honours board at Lord's with 6-84 earlier that day.

The following morning there were doubts as to whether the Test would resume. Although the game did recommence England did not even celebrate the wickets as they completed a huge innings victory to take the series.

I felt all the normal anger and indignation on being told that members of the Pakistani team had cheated in a Test match that I had been present at. With respect to the young fast bowler who was involved, Mohammad Amir, these feelings were tinged with sadness.

The three Pakistan players, including team captain Salman Butt, were all apparently involved in bowling no-balls to order so that people could bet on the next ball being a no-ball in the certain knowledge that it would come to pass. The three players in question had taken bribes from a bookmaker, Mazhar Majeed.

All three went to prison and were banned from playing cricket for five or more years. I have no sympathy for the two senior players, but Amir was just 18. He was brought up in a culture where you must respect your elders and the captain, Butt, was a man he looked up to. He made a terrible mistake, but he was little more than a kid. He knew it was wrong but did not find the courage to refuse to be involved. As a result he was left with a lifetime of regret.

Perhaps it is because I have spent my life working with children and young people that I find it hard to judge their actions as harshly as those of adults. Instead I felt sad that a young man brimming with talent would never go on to fulfil his potential. Of course he brought it upon himself, but what 18-year-old has not done something fundamentally stupid? I am aware that this is a minority opinion, but I cannot bear to think that an 18-year-old can have no way back.

It is a terrible shame that in that same match another young man, England's Stuart Broad, went a long way to establishing his credentials as a true all-rounder with his match-winning score of 169. This score was of particular significance to him as it exceeded his father Chris's highest Test match score of 162 although Chris Broad was a top-order batsman.

Is Stuart's innings devalued as a result of the spot fixing scandal? It has been argued that a bowler who goes on to the field needing to make sure he bowls the exact ball of an exact over in an illegal manner is not fully focused on his normal job of taking wickets. However, it is often forgotten that Amir bowled really well in taking six wickets and Broad and his team-mates firmly believe that it was a legitimate innings. However, it is sad for Broad that even though the results of the summer remain in the record book his greatest innings will always be tainted and when people talk about the 2010 Lord's Test match his wonderful achievement may not even get a mention.

Chapter 11

Cricket and Politics

SPORT AND politics have always been strongly linked, occasionally in a positive way but also in a way that is often quite disturbing. Going back as far as the 1936 Olympics, Adolf Hitler used the occasion to promote Aryan nationalism with his ideological belief of racial supremacy. However, he struggled to square the Nazi depiction of ethnic Africans as inferior with the performance of the black American Jesse Owens, who won gold medals in the 100m, 200m, 4×100m relay and long jump events!

In contrast, in 1968 the global stage of the Olympics was used to highlight to the world the African-American struggle during the civil rights movement in the USA. At the Games held in Mexico Tommie Smith, aged 24, won the 200m sprint final and gold medal in 19.83 seconds, the first time the 20-second barrier had been broken. His Black Power salute on the medal podium with John Carlos, who took the bronze, was a protest against racism and injustice towards African-Americans in the United States. It caused huge controversy, as it was seen as politicising the Olympic Games. It remains a symbolic moment in the history of the Black Power movement.

The 1980 Moscow Olympics became the centre of the power struggle between the Soviet Union and the West after the Soviet invasion of Afghanistan led to a boycott by America and a number of their allies.

Most famously, the sporting boycott and global isolation of South Africa played a crucial role in forcing the country to end apartheid. South Africa was excluded from the Olympics as early as 1964, and by the 1980s South Africa had also been expelled from most international sports bodies. It would appear that the international boycott of racially divided sport played a huge role in turning world opinion against the apartheid regime.

Over a much longer period cricket, whilst nobly defining itself as 'above politics', has been intertwined with international affairs from the start.

For much of its history cricket has been seen as the game that defines both the English and the British Empire. Cricket was certainly important in the attempts by the British to 'civilise' the colonies and still today it is almost exclusively these ex-colonies that play the game.

Within the Empire the spread of sport was a key element of cultural imperialism, providing an opportunity for Britain to take cultural control of her Empire, whilst also encouraging British attitudes towards class and race. Cricket was a particularly useful tool for British imperialists. In a paternalistic way, cricket allowed the British to mould the upbringing of their natives, encouraging good moral values as well as developing spirit and character.

When the game was first developing the British were of course much better cricketers as a result of their experience of playing the game. So at first British teams were likely to dominate imperial competitions, thereby demonstrating their overall superiority. However, this particular benefit was only short-lived and England's first cricketing loss at home to Australia in 1882 did real damage to the imperial self-image.

When the likes of Australia and South Africa first played cricket against England in the 19th century they were not yet established as nations and there is little doubt that the national identity derived from having their own representative cricket team accelerated their move to nationhood and also allowed the English to acknowledge them as 'nations' for the first time.

Throughout the British made sure they maintained control of the cricket rulebook and therefore, as the game became more popular, the colonies were increasingly culturally beholden to them. If sporting disputes within the colonies were to be settled, they were forced to look to the British, the guardians of the rulebook. Even today the Marylebone Cricket Club (MCC) retains copyright over the laws of the game and only MCC may change the laws, although usually this is done after consultation with the International Cricket Council (ICC).

International cricket and politics came dramatically face to face in England's 1932/33 tour to Australia, remembered as the 'Bodyline' tour.

Australia had one of the strongest batting line-ups ever in the early 1930s, which included the most prolific batsman in the history of the game, Sir Donald Bradman. In order to counter this the England captain, Douglas Jardine, backed by MCC, came up with a controversial plan wherein he instructed his two fast bowlers, Nottingham colleagues Bill Voce and Harold Larwood, to bowl at the batsman's body. He called this tactic 'fast leg theory', better known as Bodyline. The goal was to force the Australian batsmen to defend their bodies with their bats, thus providing easy catches to a stacked leg side field. Larwood was a fearsome pace bowler and using this approach he became virtually unplayable.

Australian crowds, players and administrators were incensed at the tactic and the Australian Cricket Board cabled Lord's in protest. It did not stop there as the governor of South Australia and even the Australian Prime Minister became involved.

Captain Jardine insisted that the tactic was legitimate and famously replied to the criticism with the comment, 'I've not travelled 6,000 miles to make friends. I'm here to win the Ashes.'

This row was the last thing the British government wanted and both sides were worried about the likely effect on trade and relations between Australia and the 'Mother Country'.

MCC were under pressure from both governments and started to worry that Australia would refuse to tour England in 1934. The heavily class-ridden MCC sought to apportion blame to the ex-miner Larwood rather than Winchester College old-boy Jardine. The fast bowler refused to make the apology that was called for and never played for England again. In the end MCC changed the laws of cricket-limiting the number of leg side fielders.

Relations between England and Australia are said to have remained strained until the Second World War.

* * *

As I reported earlier my brother Roy has read more about dead cricketers than the living. He is as a result of extensive reading an expert on the Bodyline tour. However, when it comes to the anti-apartheid incidents of the late 60s and early 70s involving cricket and rugby we can rely on memory and in my case memories from direct involvement.

Although they had been banned from the Olympics from 1964, opposition to South African sport was further fuelled by events in 1968 involving the cricketer Basil

D'Oliveira. Roy and I were reminded of this affair quite recently watching Notts versus Worcestershire at Trent Bridge when a young man, Brett D'Oliveira, came out to bat for Worcester. The Worcestershire fans confirmed what we suspected – that Brett is Basil's grandson.

Basil D'Oliveira was born in Cape Town in 1931 and designated as 'Cape coloured' under apartheid classification. D'Oliveira was a talented cricketer who in 1960 moved from South Africa to England primarily because the apartheid legislation seriously restricted his career prospects on racial grounds and barred him from the all-white Test team.

He qualified for Worcestershire County Cricket Club through residency in 1964 and later became a British citizen. He began his Test career with England in 1966. He played regularly for England and in 1968 was hopeful of being selected for the forthcoming tour of his homeland, South Africa. In the final Test of the English summer of 1968 (against Australia) he scored 158, apparently making sure, at least on cricketing grounds, that he would be selected. However, when the squad was announced it did not include D'Oliveira, demonstrating yet again that the 'blazers', with their colonial attitudes to life and cricket, were still very much in control.

A furore broke out in the British press and a number of Labour politicians also expressed grave concern. Both Roy and I were still living at home at the time and I remember our outrage at the decision. For some time it was almost the only topic of conversation in our house. When a player originally selected, Tom Cartwright, dropped out due to injury D'Oliveira was subsequently chosen for the tour as the cricketing authorities finally bowed to public pressure. It was always known that the South African government would not accept a team including a coloured South African and they duly intervened to cancel the tour.

Unperturbed, MCC went on to invite South Africa to tour England in 1970 and it was at this point that the Stop the Seventy Tour committee formed and promised to bring disruption to any match the tourists might play.

The Stop the Seventy Tour committee (STST) used non-violent civil disobedience and direct action on a scale the world of sport had never seen before. Focused mainly on the 1969/70 South African rugby tour, it was a campaign that successfully halted the white South African cricket tour of England in 1970 which, according to STST, was always their goal. This represents a famous victory over racism in general and the apartheid nature of South African sport in particular.

The Anti-Apartheid Movement and STST organised demonstrations and direct action at every match played by the Springbok rugby team on its tour of Britain. Peter Hain, later a cabinet minister in Tony Blair's Labour government, was then a Young Liberal. A native of South Africa from a white family who had been forced into exile in Britain because of his parents' opposition to apartheid, he became the de facto leader of the campaign.

Hain believed that when the anti-apartheid struggle was only on the news pages it could be dismissed by white South Africans, but when it stopped their sport it hit them hard. They could deal with being shunned by other nations politically as long as their cricket and rugby teams could compete around the world. Ironically, their defence was that sport and politics don't mix!

I had just started at university and, much as I loved cricket and rugby, I despised racism and enthusiastically embraced the campaign. I took part in two demonstrations at Twickenham, for the first match of the Springbok tour against Oxford University and later for the Test against England. I was still playing rugby and was a fan through and through, but my love of the game was not shaken by these events. This was not the case for everyone and one of my abiding memories was the flack I got from comrades because it mattered to me that England won the game! The scenes were chaotic and, I'm glad to say, put the wind up the cricket establishment as well as their rugby counterparts.

Having witnessed the scenes at the rugby matches around the country the cricket authorities knew they faced widespread disruption and as a direct result the 1970 South Africa cricket tour was scrapped. This heralded the start of a worldwide boycott of South African teams and athletes in sports including football and cricket, finally catching up with the position taken by the International Olympic Committee in 1964. This sporting boycott lasted for 25 years.

As a cricket fan I was, of course, sad to see how badly the authorities handled the crisis of racism at the time, having to be dragged kicking and screaming to the eventual adoption of anti-apartheid policies. However, although this made me extremely angry it never altered my love of the game. I had been brought up in a very different environment in which cricket was seen as the people's sport. My father and his friends, who gathered each weekend at the local public playing fields, believed this passionately and I took my lead from them.

These men had recently fought a war and they were all part of the political movement of the time that demanded a wide set of rights for working people and access to sport and leisure was central to this.

As a young undergraduate I was also part of a new political wave that emanated from the civil rights protests in America and grew under the shadow of the Vietnam war. It was a movement that supported and gave courage to public protest across the Western world with the values of equality, justice and peace at its heart. It was within this framework that the anti-apartheid demonstrations that I was involved in took place. American folk musicians, like Bob Dylan, Phil Ochs and Tom Paxton, provided the anthems as music became integral to this movement.

The central notion was that the world and its resources belonged to everyone, not a privileged few, and I applied this approach to everything I was involved in. So back to cricket, this reinforced my belief that the game should be administered by an independent body that encouraged access rather than exclusivity and supported everyone irrespective of race or gender who wanted to play the game.

At the time the governing body of English cricket was a male only club, Marylebone Cricket Club (MCC), founded in 1787. The club's tendency to select teams based on social class lasted into the 60s and its determination to keep women out of the club lasted until 1998. However, in the meantime its administrative and governance functions had been transferred to the England and Wales Cricket Board (ECB).

The ECB, in contrast to MCC, has done much to encourage women and black and ethnic minorities to get involved in cricket and this is reflected in the modern game.

The struggles to create equal opportunities and make cricket a truly accessible sport go on, but are merely a reflection of the same struggles for equality of opportunity that continue in Britain as a whole.

Away from cricket, racism in sport is far from eradicated. With the rise of the far right in Europe the awful spectacle of racist chanting has returned to our football grounds. One can only hope it will be dealt with effectively.

Chapter 12

The Innings of a Batting Genius

AS AN ex-fast bowler I confess to being more interested in performances with the ball than with the bat. That much can probably be ascertained from everything I have written thus far.

Watching Stuart Broad take eight wickets for 15 runs at Trent Bridge remains the most exhilarating experience I have ever had watching cricket, made even more memorable because it was the Ashes.

In his autobiography, *Bowl, Sleep, Repeat*, Jimmy Anderson makes a good case for cricket always being on the side of the batsman.

'Every single conceivable law in cricket is devised so that it suits the batsman. If there is any doubt, *any* doubt at all, the batsman will always receive the benefit … If we were at war in ancient times we'd be the boulder carriers.'[3]

Anderson was certainly not the first person to express this sentiment. In 1903 in his book *Cricket*, Gilbert Jessop complained about the very same imbalance.

'The undue prominence bestowed on batting is in a large measure accountable for the dearth of good bowlers. To set a batsman who has scored 50 runs on a good wicket on the same level with the bowler, who may have caused the dismissal of half the side, is unfair to the latter.' [7]

Jessop was complaining about the custom amongst county clubs to award a guinea as talent money to any professional who scores 50 runs, and the same sum to a bowler taking five wickets.

'To score 50 runs is a simple matter indeed compared with the task of disposing of half a side, and it therefore stands to reason that a bowler who may possess some little talent as a batsman will endeavour to cultivate his batting, even at the expense of his bowling, when he sees it is manifestly to his advantage to do so.' [7]

It seems that the sport was tilted towards batsmen even at that point. Another contributor to the same book, Charlie Townsend, a Gloucestershire and England all-rounder, seems to agree.

'There is no question that the general run of wickets that are played upon today are immensely superior [for batting] to what they were even ten years ago ... and it is hard to say where you will meet with a bad wicket in County cricket.'[7]

Townsend also had something to say about the ever-improving bats.

'The bats themselves have improved to a great extent. Every year they seem to bring out better bats, and to make them with better balance, better handles, and generally better shape.'[7]

In other words, there is nothing new about batsmen gaining undue advantage in cricket. It has always been there, as bats and wickets have improved over time and protective gear has arrived.

In recent years the popularity of limited-overs cricket has only accelerated the process. With games largely played on flat wickets using a white ball with less propensity to swing, scores have got higher and the lot of the bowler even tougher. Commonly pace bowlers have to suffer the ignominy of seeing an average of six or seven runs scored off each over.

You would think that Ian Botham, probably England's most entertaining player, would as an all-rounder have an open mind to this question, but he has regularly expressed the same sentiment as Anderson. I have to agree with them. My view is that no one works as hard as the pace bowler and for me seeing the middle stump cartwheeling behind the bewildered batsman is not only just reward for all the hard work, but also the greatest thrill in cricket whether watching or playing.

Nevertheless, there are some individual batting performances that I will never forget. Clearly Botham's two innings in 1981 against Australia are up there as is Stokes's in 2019 at Leeds also against the Aussies. However, the best I have ever seen was Kevin Pietersen, again at Leeds, playing for England in 2012 against the country of his birth, South Africa.

It had been a warm August, even in Leeds, but Roy and I arrived on the Friday during a chilly second day with tickets for days three and four. We had settled into our campsite about 12 miles from the ground, but crucially with a pub doing food within walking distance. As we sat over a pint on the Friday night we discussed the progress of the match so far.

England had won the toss and made the somewhat surprising decision to put South Africa in to bat. It had soon looked like a mistake as the two openers reached 120 without loss early on day one. South Africa had continued to bat until tea on the second day, making a first innings score of 419, thereby ensuring England would always be chasing the game. With some help from bad light and then rain England's opening batsmen, Strauss and Cook, had negotiated a tricky last session with their wickets intact. So our cricket would start on day three with England still needing 371 to achieve first innings parity. Rather optimistically we concluded that the game was well set up.

. As was now our well-established habit we arrived at the ground on Saturday morning about an hour before play was due to resume. The weather had changed for the better and there was no reason not to expect a good performance from our team.

Emily and Andy had quite recently lived in Leeds, Emily having studied at the university for her PhD. She knew the ground well as she had been a member of Yorkshire CCC for two or three seasons. However, now living back in North Wales, their cricket excursions had been severely curtailed by the birth of their two children. Nevertheless, given it was Leeds they managed to enlist Andy's parents as babysitters for the day and we were due to meet them at the ground.

As was now *their* well-established habit, they arrived five minutes before the start of play looking hot and bothered. In fairness to Andrew this had been Emily's modus operandi for most of her life. Their seats were in the same stand as ours, ten yards along and three or four rows behind. After a short time Andy and I swapped seats so I could have a chat with Emily. Looking down on Roy and Andy it would have made a great photo. Roy, still stuck in yesterday's weather, had on a short overcoat and scarf, a leather cap and heavy boots whereas Andy, sitting alongside him, wore T-shirt and shorts and flip-flops. As Roy said, it's best to be prepared!

The innings did not start well for England, who lost Alastair Cook for just 24 before a rain delay vindicated Roy's preparedness and made a sucker of Andy in his shirt and shorts. After lunch England lost more quick wickets, leaving them still 246 behind at 173/4. If we were to have any chance in this match something needed to happen, and soon.

It did. Pietersen and debutant James Taylor put on a century partnership to which Taylor contributed only 20 runs although he showed admirable resistance as his partner ran amok at the other end.

Earlier Pietersen had signalled his intentions by getting off the mark with successive pull shots to the boundary off Dale Steyn bowling at 90mph. Later, after Pietersen had caused carnage against the rest of the strong South African bowling attack, the captain Graeme Smith brought Steyn back to try and stem the tide. Immediately Pietersen launched the world's fastest bowler straight down the ground for a magnificent six. Roy and I, now sitting together again, had a perfect view as Steyn passed his captain on the way back to his mark. He looked at Smith and shrugged as if to say, 'I haven't a clue what to do next.'

It was a thrilling day for England supporters, with Pietersen showing arrogance and confidence in equal measure in the way he went after South Africa's world-renowned fast bowlers. Several times he used the 'flamingo', a thrilling cricket shot of his own invention, executed standing on one leg and swivelling on the front foot. I don't think I have ever seen an innings like it and do not expect to in the future.

After the day's play Emily and Andy headed home as Andy's parents were looking after the kids whereas Roy and I had a shower and headed for the pub.

We had been so consumed with the cricket we had not given the Olympics much thought, but when we arrived at the pub everyone was gathered around the TV waiting for the final event of the heptathlon. One of the locals who we had been chatting with the night before soon brought us up to speed with the news that Team GB had won gold in the rowing and the cycling, but now everyone's attention was on Jessica Ennis in the 800m race of the heptathlon.

It was already pretty likely that Jess Ennis would win heptathlon gold. She had put herself in a dominant position in the morning's long jump and the javelin. She was almost there.

However, as the 800m started the roar from the crowd was as if she had to win that race too in order to take gold. The crowd was screaming, as was everyone in the pub, as the bell indicating a lap left rang out with Jess in the lead. Then with 200 metres to go she was overtaken first by Lilli Schwarzkopf and then Tatiana Chernova. This was one of Schwarzkopf's best events and it would not have affected the medal positions had she won.

But it mattered to the crowd and suddenly it seemed like life and death to Jessica Ennis. This was her Games, and she was not going to let it happen. When she kicked again and regained the lead the crowd went wild, as did our group huddled around a TV set 200 miles from the action. She threw her head back and closed her eyes as she crossed the line in front. The 2012 poster girl had pulled off a remarkable feat driven on by the power of her home crowd.

'Super Saturday' was completed by Greg Rutherford winning the long jump gold and Mo Farah coming home in front to win the 10,000m final. For Roy and me this topped off one of the most exciting days a sports fan could ever have dreamt of.

Pietersen's brilliance completely changed the complexion of the match, bringing England back into the game. He was out almost immediately the next morning for 149 and Roy and I joined in the rousing standing ovation, although in truth we felt profound disappointment that this amazing innings had come to an end.

The game finished in a draw with honours pretty well even. Ultimately it was a shame that, with several rain breaks throughout the match, such a fine innings was not quite enough to engineer a victory.

It is hard to believe that as a result of issues off the field Pietersen was dropped for the next Test. Although he did play again, against India, New Zealand and then Australia he was eventually sacked by England in 2014 and never played international cricket after that.

Before the series started Pietersen had announced his retirement from 50-over one-day international cricket. Although he still wanted to play Twenty20 matches for England, the terms of his central contract meant that he had to retire from both forms, remaining available for Test cricket only.

After the second Test Pietersen surprised the cricketing public by suggesting the third and final Test of that series could be his last. Clearly something was afoot and, in the same press conference, he mentioned issues within the dressing room that needed to be resolved. In the following days, allegations were made that he had sent text messages to members of the South African dressing room, insulting Andrew Strauss, England's captain, and Andy Flower the coach.

Following talks with the ECB, Pietersen then unreservedly committed his future to all forms of cricket for England in a video interview posted on YouTube. However, he was dropped for the third Test after failing to provide clarification about the text messages, despite the announcement of the squad being delayed to give him more time to do so.

In October 2012, the ECB confirmed that they had a process which could open the way for Pietersen's return to the team and indeed this led to his selection for the Test squad to tour India. It was a successful tour for England and for Pietersen, who scored 338 runs in four Tests including a century and two fifties.

Pietersen featured in the three-Test series in New Zealand in February 2013, scoring 73 in the second match. A knee injury forced him to miss the return home series in May that year, but he was fit again in time for the 2013 Ashes series. On 3 August 2013 Pietersen not only scored a century in the third Ashes Test, he became the highest run scorer for England across all forms of cricket combined.

His return Ashes tour in 2013/14 was less successful. In a series which England lost 5-0, Pietersen averaged only 29 and passed fifty only twice in ten innings. However, to put his performance in context he was still England's leading scorer with 294 runs. The fallout from the tour led to the removal of Flower as head coach, and there was much media speculation about the nature of Pietersen's relationship with the team management.

The ECB met and announced on 4 February 2014 that Pietersen had not been selected for the upcoming tour of the Caribbean, a decision they described as 'unanimous'. The media speculated that Pietersen's career was over and so it proved. At that time Pietersen was, in my humble opinion, still England's best batsman and if judged on purely cricket terms would have continued for several years.

For cricket lovers this was hard to take. There is no doubt that Pietersen was very difficult to be around and his behaviour in what became known as 'textgate' required some form of censure. However, to allow his career to end prematurely is unforgivable.

Most contemporary cricketers, including those that fell out with him, acknowledge that he was one of the greatest batsmen of his generation. Many refer to him as a batting genius and the innings at Headingley I described confirms that. Surely his eccentricities should have been managed.

People with rare sporting talent are not always easy to get along with. They usually march to the beat of their own drum and don't go out of their way to fit in. Their behaviours can often be seen as eccentric and, as with Pietersen, sometimes unacceptable. Often they reach the pinnacle of their sport through an obsessive dedication to improving their talent. All successful sporting competitors are, by necessity, focused, driven, confident and determined to succeed. For those who are exceptionally talented the drive and the focus may be particularly strong and sometimes, although by no means always, this results in behaviour that might be described as egoistic, arrogant or self-obsessed.

Muhammad Ali, widely regarded as the greatest heavyweight boxer of all time, was often described in these terms. Certainly Ali had a tremendous ego, but not the ego we might associate with many lesser boxers. Ali's statement early in his career that he was indeed the greatest was not empty self-importance, but ego born from a true belief that he could do things others could not. However, a boxer is a lone sportsman and 'fitting in' is not an imperative as it may be in team sports.

Golf is another game based on individual skill and top golfers are often obsessive about their form and their scores. The greatest golfer of the current generation, Tiger Woods, has won 15 major championships, putting him second in the all-time list. Winning a major is only about individual performance, but Woods' record when playing as part of a team in the Ryder Cup is far less impressive. In fact he has lost far more matches than he has won.

You cannot be a successful soccer or rugby player if you do not play for the team as success comes only through collective effort. Cricket is a halfway house. It is a team sport dominated by individual performances and so there is a place for those highly talented cricketers who are obsessed with their own performance, albeit an uncomfortable one. Ian Botham and Geoffrey Boycott were rare talents notoriously hard to manage but are two of the greatest English cricketers of all time.

Those with exceptional talent come with baggage and sometimes their behaviour is hard to deal with, but to fail to find ways to get the best out of them is to fail their chosen art. I find it hard to forgive the cricketing authorities for depriving me and Roy, and other cricket lovers, of more innings from Pietersen like the one we witnessed at Headingley.

Chapter 13

Nottinghamshire County Cricket Club and Us

IN THE summer of 2013 Roy and I, having watched only international cricket for far too long, decided to reacquaint ourselves with the very different joys of the county game.

We had been brought up as Middlesex supporters, that being the cricket club our dad followed, but in all honesty it had never been a strong affiliation.

Although cricket was the game our father loved most, first and foremost he liked playing and that always took priority. So, with the exception of a few Test matches against the West Indies or Australia, most of his cricket watching was done at home in front of the telly and so it was with us. Our support of Middlesex was therefore confined to looking for their scores first when the paper boy poked the newspaper through the door and prioritising Middlesex players when collecting and swapping cricket cards.

It was different when it came to football. Our dad took us to Stamford Bridge regularly and we were ardent Chelsea fans by the age of six or seven. Although they have been a strong team throughout the Premier League period it was very different in the 1950s and 60s. I once told my dad that making us Chelsea supporters at that time could almost be construed as child abuse.

Later in life Roy and I both took what opportunities presented themselves to watch some county cricket. For me that meant an annual visit to Colwyn Bay Cricket Club where Glamorgan play one match each year and Roy satisfied himself with occasional minor counties matches watching Norfolk play at Horsford's beautiful Manor Park ground.

Choosing where to go for our return to county cricket was relatively easy. Trent Bridge had for some time been our favourite ground and we had enjoyed some memorable Test matches there. Also, with Roy living in Norfolk and me in North Wales it was pretty well equidistant, or one could say mutually inconvenient, for each of us.

Nottinghamshire has always been an ambitious club although surprisingly, given they are a top county, Notts has won the County Championship only six times in 130 years. Compare this to Yorkshire (33), Surrey (20), Middlesex (13) and Lancashire (9). However, they have achieved considerable success in recent years in the shorter forms of the game, winning the T20 Blast again in 2020. Although this has not yet transferred to their Championship form, they have a competent and ambitious coach in Peter Moores who has won the County Championship with two of his previous clubs, Sussex and Lancashire.

However, none of this played any role in our decision to embrace Notts and Trent Bridge. In this decision the love of the game was uppermost, not our hopes and aspirations for success, although we do harbour some. It was the history and heritage that is attached to Notts and to their wonderful ground that drew us.

Roy and I had no intention of just turning up like two waifs or strays; instead we planned our first sortie with military precision. We had decided to watch at least three days of cricket and so our first move was to book a campsite. Over the years watching Test matches at Trent Bridge we had tried out just about every site within striking distance of the ground, but the one that met our needs best was the well-appointed Thornton's Holt campsite in the small hamlet of Stragglethorpe.

In nearby Radcliffe-on-Trent there were two small supermarkets, a chippy and an excellent pub, the Chestnut, serving food and about eight different real ales. Whether the pub was within walking distance was a constant 'discussion' between Roy and me. Usually we did walk back to the site, but if we didn't quite have the energy there was a bus that would get us most of the way back.

We agreed to get to the site the afternoon before the match and, as if to underline the precise planning, we arrived from opposite directions at the exact same moment!

On the first day we were really excited and we got to the ground more than an hour before the game equipped with doughnuts to go with our morning coffee, the start of an enduring ritual. The contrast with a Test match was total. Our tickets allowed us to sit anywhere other than the members'-only pavilion and, except for small clusters of spectators sat behind the bowler's arm, we had a choice of anywhere in the ground. The only thing to hold us back was the feeling that the Nottingham stalwarts were likely to have their regular seats. In the end we settled about three rows back in the Radcliffe Road Stand in easy reach of the coffee kiosk.

As the players took the field it seemed as if we had been transported back to the late 1950s. There was no singing of 'Jerusalem', no chants or verbal encouragement of any sort and no players' huddle, just gentle, polite applause. The players immediately took up their fielding positions, the umpire took his arm away from the bowler's run-up and called 'play', and we were off.

We sat there completely absorbed as the cricket progressed at its own leisurely pace and we became drawn into the soothing rhythm of the day. Lunch when it came was not a break from the frenetic action of a Test match, but an event in itself. Roy, who had taken a meander around the ground before play, had discovered an excellent and very reasonable restaurant at the top of the Radcliffe Road Stand that was not open to the public during international matches. There we ate a very pleasant lunch with an excellent pint of Guinness.

There was a TV in the corner showing live international cricket from somewhere around the globe, but we had no interest in it. We had found what we came for. In just two hours our love of county cricket had been rekindled and we have never looked back.

For the next two years our return to watching county cricket was put on hold as my wife and I went to live abroad. In our second year away, 2015, I did come home for a week to watch the Ashes at Trent Bridge, but it was 2016 before Roy and I assembled for another dose of county cricket.

We watched four or five Championship matches which we really enjoyed. In the first game we watched at Trent Bridge Notts beat a strong Surrey team. Steven Mullaney scored an excellent 113 in the first innings and a five-wicket haul from Jake Ball later in the game was ultimately enough to sink Surrey, although not before Notts had suffered a near fatal middle order collapse, something we were to get used to. However, it was ultimately a disappointing season for Notts, who ended up relegated from the first division of the County Championship after nine years in the top flight.

As the 2017 season approached we had a decision to make. Almost by accident we had become confirmed Nottinghamshire fans although they had provided us with only sporadic encouragement. They were now in the second division and if we were serious about supporting county cricket and Notts in particular we needed to become members. It made economic sense too. A year's senior membership cost just over £100, giving admission to all home games and priority for international cricket tickets. We willingly signed up.

For both of us, but particularly for Roy, this opened up a whole new world. Consistent with his now well chronicled love of dead cricketers, his attention immediately centred on the museum and the library. Nottingham has a rich cricket history which is well documented in these two fine institutions.

The first documented game of cricket in Nottingham took place at The Forest between Nottingham and Sheffield. Unfortunately, it ended in a fist fight and neither the result of the game nor of the brawl is recorded. By 1830, William Clarke, landlord of The Bell Inn, had developed a side that beat Sheffield and Leicester and later Cambridge and Sussex, the latter taking three days to travel up to Nottingham by stagecoach, only to get thrashed.

In 1836 a North vs South game was staged in Leicester rather than in Nottingham, despite North featuring nine Nottinghamshire players. The ground in Leicester was enclosed, which meant they could charge to get in, whereas games at The Forest were free. This clearly gave William Clarke, now married to the landlady of the Trent Bridge Inn, an idea. In 1838, he put up a fence around the field at the back of the pub and made a cricket ground. For the rest of that century Notts were consistently in the top two or three sides in the country.

In 1899 Trent Bridge hosted its first Test match, between England and Australia. However, the first international to be played there was a football match between England

Wheel of Brisbane, built in 2008 to celebrate the 150th anniversary of the State of Queensland.

First Ashes Test 2006 at Brisbane. Me travelling to the cricket by ferry

Inside the Gabba on day one, First Ashes Test 2006. Being used to cricket grounds in England, it was a lot to take in.

The Regatta Bar, Brisbane, quickly established as our local, offering great food and beer sold in huge jugs. Image by Marzena Photography

A little worse for wear at the Pig and Whistle, Brisbane. In my quest for good beer I finally tried a Guinness but couldn't detect the Dublin taste.

Paddy Powell, Charlton Athletic legend and junior cricketer [Tony (Reckless) Hammond]

Fourth Ashes Test 2005 at Trent Bridge: Ashley Giles celebrates the winning runs

Fourth Ashes Test 2015 at Trent Bridge. Even Broad can't believe it as an amazing catch by Stokes gives him another wicket on his way to 8-15.

MCC members who governed cricket until 1993

Entrance to Thornton's Holt Campsite in Stragglethorpe, Nottinghamshire.

Roy with his beloved VW campervan, 'Dorothy'

Our luxurious overnight accommodation in Nottinghamshire

Kandy, Sri Lanka November 2018

Day/night match at the magnificent Trent Bridge, home of Notts CCC and Test match venue. [Notts CCC]

My grandchildren, Iris and Finlay at Sophia Gardens, Cardiff. Mascots for the first World Cup game to be played in Wales – New Zealand vs Sri Lanka, 2019

Jos Buttler of England celebrates running out Martin Guptill of New Zealand to seal victory for England in the final of the ICC Cricket World Cup 2019

The Barmy Army in full voice during the first Ashes Test match between Australia and England at the Gabba on 27 November 2006.

Australian player Brett Lee fields in front of the chanting Barmy Army on the final day of the first Ashes Test match, in Brisbane on 27 November 2006.

Taking in the sights around Capetown on New Year's Day 2020

South Africa versus England second Test at Newlands, Cape Town in January 2020. Lunch on day two with Table Mountain in the background

South Africa versus England second Test at Newlands, day four. On our way to the ground we were reluctantly led across the railway line as the underpass was flooded.

South Africa versus England second Test at Newlands, Cape Town in January 2020, day five. Savouring a hard-fought victory.

August 1989: England wicketkeeper Jack Russell in action during the sixth Test against Australia at the Oval.

International friendly – England v Colombia at Wembley September 1995. Rene Higuita, Colombia's goalie, clears the ball with a backward overhead kick.

My cricket-loving grandson, Finlay at the Trent Bridge pavilion August 2018

England versus India August 2018 at Trent Bridge. Joe Root giving his autograph to Fin while I look down to avoid being starstruck.

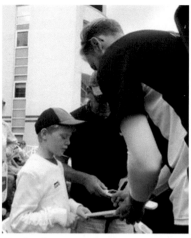

England versus India August 2018 at Trent Bridge. Stuart Broad giving Fin his autograph. How tall is that guy?

England versus India August 2018 at Trent Bridge. Fin's bat with the autographs of his heroes.

Finlay, proudly wearing his North Wales kit

Finlay and Iris, on whom we rely to hand on their love of cricket, the gift left to my brother and me by our dad

and Ireland in 1897. Hockey, lacrosse and tennis also featured and there used to be a cinder running track around the ground.

Over the years the whole ground has been redeveloped and that continues. The pavilion is thankfully one of the few parts of the ground that has not been updated. During the First World War, the building was used as a hospital for injured soldiers.

A.W. Shelton, a retired estate agent, spent most of his time watching cricket at Trent Bridge and in 1938, the club's centenary, he asked people to bring in memorabilia and these items remained on display in the long room in the pavilion until the late 70s. Around this time a full set of *Wisden Almanacks* were presented to Notts and in 1977 a benefactor left about 8,000 books to the club. That was when the library was officially started, housed in a room in the main pavilion. The current museum opened in 1988.

Today, there are more than 17,000 books in the Trent Bridge library which until his death in 2021 was run by former president Peter Wynne-Thomas.

To observe Roy and me in attendance at a county game you would think that he had been a member for 40 years and I was his guest for the day. He appears to know half the locals intimately and to be at least on nodding terms with everyone else. He holds long conversations with the very civil and extremely knowledgeable groundstaff who even acknowledge him when seen out and about in the city. He is often quite overcome with the sheer joy of being a member. He is perfectly suited to county cricket, in his words 'so less fraught than the high drama of the Tests'.

The 2017 season, our first as members, was richly entertaining and highly successful. Following relegation the previous year, changes were made in the coaching set-up with Peter Moores taking over as head coach. Moores

CRICKET, MY BROTHER AND ME

assured supporters that, 'One-day cricket and player development were key priorities, alongside the ultimate aim of promotion.'

Captain Chris Read, who had been at the club for 20 years, announced that he would retire at the end of the season. Unusually Notts had their England bowlers Stuart Broad and Jake Ball available and they were joined by Australian fast bowler James Pattinson. This potent bowling attack proved to be far too good for second division opponents and the season started with three excellent Championship victories. Roy and I were in heaven.

On our next visit to Trent Bridge we saw Notts easily beat Gloucestershire by an innings. A number of frustrating draws followed before Notts demolished Leicestershire for the second time with stalwart Samit Patel scoring 247.

On Monday, 26 June 2017 Notts played their first day-night Championship game with a pink ball against Kent. All other county games took place at the same time and under the same conditions. Roy and I did not go to this match, but followed it with interest and some disquiet.

The truth is we ardently hoped the experiment would fail. The idea arose primarily to allow England players to acclimatise to the ball and conditions prior to a planned day-night Test match against the West Indies later in the season. However, the counties were also interested in whether it would positively affect the number of spectators.

We had now established a very pleasant pattern around home county matches. We would travel to Nottingham on the morning of the first day, meeting at the ground. Each evening we would get back to the campsite around six, have a shower and head to Radcliffe for a few pints and a meal. We would spend three nights at the campsite and at the end of the final day would head home in our separate directions. It was not just the cricket we loved, the whole 'package' was very enjoyable. If the game started at 2pm and went on until 9pm our established pattern would be completely ruined.

On the evening of the first day I remember seeing a photo on the internet of a Notts player, Luke Fletcher, fielding in the deep. To my horror I saw a huge crowd behind him, my worst nightmare. As it turned out this was just the novelty value of the first day-night Championship game. In the event, the attendance was no higher across the four days than normal and therefore the county had no reason to consider day-night matches as the future. This was a great relief to us both.

In the game a victory for Notts looked inevitable as they dominated from the start, but rain intervened with Notts requiring just 75 in their second innings. Another draw.

Notts had led the division for the entire season but consecutive defeats against promotion rivals Worcestershire and then Northants meant at least a draw was needed in the final game at Hove to gain the second promotion spot. Sussex batted first and scored 565. In reply, Notts were 65/5 and seemed doomed to miss out on promotion, but thanks to a 242 partnership between Joe Root's younger brother Billy and retiring captain and club legend Chris Read, they recovered. Read scored 124 in his final match to ensure his team's promotion back to Division One at the first time of asking. A fairy tale end to a great career.

In fact, all three priorities set out by the new head coach Peter Moores were achieved with victories in both the 50-over and the Twenty20 finals, promotion to Division One and the introduction of young players.

The following season, 2018, was one of two halves. At the halfway point Notts were sitting in top spot, but after that they lost five of the remaining six matches, just about avoiding a return to Division Two. In 2019 Notts did get relegated again, going the whole season without a win. For two now committed fans it was hard to take.

Both Roy and I love the tradition whereby first-class county teams play at outgrounds. As mentioned earlier I have for many years enjoyed first-class cricket at Colwyn Bay Cricket Club, just 20 miles from my home, where Glamorgan play one first-class match each year. So when we heard that Nottinghamshire were due to play their first ever first-class fixture at Welbeck CC beginning on Sunday, 9 June 2019 we decided to go along. The four-day County Championship match was to be against Hampshire.

Welbeck Cricket Club is set in picturesque surroundings in Sookholme, near Mansfield in the north of the county. The club had made a real effort and when we arrived for the first day the ground looked glorious. There is a grass bank around most of the perimeter of the playing area and so on a nice day you could just sit on the grass to watch. However, the club had set up deckchairs close to the boundary rope and some people, including us, had brought their own camping chairs.

Pristine white marquees had been erected around the ground adorned by bright flags billowing in the wind, drawing the eye to their vivid colours. Bunting decorated the entrances intended to entice the spectators in to sample the excellent catering. Tantalising aromas of pies and pasties, jacket potatoes and sugary doughnuts wafted across the ground. There was also an inviting clubhouse bar. All was perfectly set up for a great occasion.

When it came to the cricket, it was much more disappointing with Notts, batting first, only able to reach 162, with Mullaney's 45 the nearest thing to a decent score. By the close Hampshire had reached 93 for the loss of just two wickets.

There was a really good crowd in and it's interesting how the atmosphere and dynamics change when the spectators are sitting just beyond the boundary rope. At once a healthy repartee was established between the players and those watching. The Australian pace bowler James Pattinson, who was at the time still the Notts overseas player, was fielding on the boundary right where Roy and I were sitting. His wife, Kayla, was also there with their young daughter and they appeared to be discussing domestic matters between deliveries. Kayla was sporting a pair of designer jeans with holes in the knees. One of the Welbeck crowd could not resist a comment.

'Blimey, Patto, on your wages surely you could buy the girl a decent pair of kecks!'

Although disappointed by Notts' first day performance, Roy and I were looking forward to the rest of the match at such a warm and intimate venue. We had booked into an excellent inn, the Dukeries Lodge in Edwinstowe just seven miles away, and everything was set fair. Then that night the heavens opened and it hardly stopped raining for the next three days. The game was completely washed out.

We so felt for the Welbeck club who not only had to bear the loss of a high prestige fixture for which they had prepared so immaculately, but also, I assume, a massive loss of revenue. The British weather had struck again.

Ever the optimist, despite a terrible season in 2019, I still expected Notts, with their exciting young squad, to come good again and they have. In their matches in 2021, following the break enforced by Covid 19, they have suddenly looked like a balanced outfit. In terms of our commitment, it makes no difference. Whatever happens now or in the future, my expectation is that we will both remain members at Nottinghamshire County Cricket Club for the rest of our lives.

Chapter 14

The Moon Under Water

I MENTIONED earlier that over the years Roy and I have tried out just about every campsite within range of Trent Bridge. This is also true of the many trips we have made to both Headingley and Old Trafford. I am not certain how we arrived at the decision to always stay at campsites, but it seems to have become our preferred option.

In particular, I am not a great lover of bed and breakfast. I live halfway up a Welsh mountain with a German wife who hates small talk and a bunch of horses so I'm not at my most chatty in the morning. When I am away at the cricket all I want to do is to sit and talk to Roy about the prospects for the day's play. If the tables are well spaced out and a self-service buffet breakfast is provided I am fine. If however I am forced to chat to other guests then I can get quite desperate.

Staying in a pub can often be suitably anonymous, but an overnighter in a pub presents Roy with a different set of problems altogether. Roy ran public houses for the best part of 20 years, often providing accommodation and meals and he ran a tight ship. To sit in the middle of a chaotic bar, still not cleared up from the night before, trying to enjoy his breakfast is the stuff of nightmares for him. I am relieved to report that this antipathy towards pubs does not extend to drinking in them.

I guess we decided to give campsites a try when Roy first bought himself a vintage 1970 VW camper van and although the sleeping arrangements were a bit tight for two big blokes we enjoyed the experience in every other way. Roy still owns the camper van, now with a huge awning, as well as a trailer tent and I have a small caravan. We tend to rotate between these different options.

I said earlier that the campsite near Trent Bridge that best meets our needs is Thornton's Holt in the hamlet of Stragglethorpe, but before settling on that we had a number of interesting experiences.

Our first camping trip to watch England at Trent Bridge was in 1998. England had found South Africa to be tough opponents since their readmission to Test cricket. England had drawn the home series in 1994 and then lost in South Africa two years later. We were due to watch the fourth Test with England already 1-0 down with only two Tests to play. They had to win this game to stay in the series. Incidentally, it was in this match that Andrew Flintoff made his Test debut aged only 20.

We had tickets for Saturday and Sunday and had booked a pitch in a campsite near Nottingham located in the grounds of a hotel. We arrived on Friday afternoon and spent a quiet evening in the hotel bar before turning in early. However, before going to bed I had got it into my head that there was a pub where we could get a last drink just along the A52 around the first bend. In the pitch black and with no pedestrian path or even a grass verge I insisted that we set off along one of the busiest A-roads in Britain. Eventually Roy refused to go any further and I was forced to surrender the pilgrimage just 100 yards short of our goal, or so I believed. On the way to the ground the next morning we discovered the 'pub' was about four miles away and had been converted to an Indian restaurant.

On day one England captain, Alec Stewart, had surprised everyone by putting South Africa in and they had responded with a first innings score of 374, built around a fine century by their skipper, Hansie Cronje. On Friday England had got themselves back into the match, posting 202/4 by close of play. The Saturday, our first day, looked like being a very important day.

We were up early the following morning and in the ground by ten ready for what turned out to be an intriguing day's cricket. By the close of play the two sides were evenly placed.

To avoid spending the whole evening in the hotel bar, we had a couple of pints on the way home, sat around at the campsite for a few hours and finally went over to the hotel for a nightcap at about 10.30pm.

There were only three people in the bar. One never expects to find much atmosphere in a hotel bar and with so few people it was particularly quiet. We both ordered a pint of Guinness, as no real ale was available, trying not to notice the price. As we got deeper into conversation the Guinness seemed to be slipping down. All the time we had been there we could hear music from a nearby room. We had not paid it much attention up until then, but as the three other occupants of our bar wished us goodnight and the barman began clearing tables and yawning, we decided to follow the music and see what was going on.

We soon found ourselves in a large room with a four-piece band playing in the corner. The room was packed and some couples were dancing. Not sure quite what we had walked into, we decided to get ourselves a couple of pints of Guinness and see what happened.

'I'm not sure we should be here,' said Roy, although it didn't stop him ordering the beer. 'It's obviously some sort of private party. Everyone's very smart.'

However, my mind was made up. 'I'm not sure what it is, but as long as the bar stays open we stay. I'm starting to enjoy this Guinness.'

Soon more people got up to dance. As a young woman in a white dress and a veil pulled back from her face joined them there was no longer any doubt as to what we had gate-crashed!

Roy was starting to show the effects of the Guinness, but I decided some chivalrous behaviour was called for. As the bride left her dance partner and wandered off to talk to a group of friends I went to speak to her.

'I'm really sorry. My brother and I came over from the hotel bar not knowing it was a wedding. We'll drink up and go.'

'Not on my account,' she replied. 'Stay as long as you want. There are about 20 people here I've never met before so two more won't make any difference!'

The bride had a delightful Irish accent which caused me some surprise that she did not have an Irish band. I said this to her.

'Just wait until the last session. They've promised the full works. We might even get "Danny Boy"!'

I thanked her profusely for her hospitality, but she waved my thanks away.

'There's plenty of food left if you want some. Help yourselves.'

I went back over to Roy with a huge grin on my face. I couldn't wait to give him the good news.

'Gosh, how nice. She's gorgeous, isn't she?' he said, doing his best to focus.

Roy's timing with women had never been good, but to have amorous thoughts about someone who had been married that morning seemed particularly ill-judged. About 20 minutes later the bride sought us out to check we were okay. We weren't hard to find as we still hadn't moved from the bar. We were chatting amiably when a young guy approached her in an urgent manner.

'Give me a minute, I'm just getting to know our new guests,' she said in response.

'I think we need to do it now,' he insisted, although it wasn't clear to me what he wanted.

'I said just give me a minute and I'll be over.'

Ever gallant, Roy decided a chivalrous intervention was called for.

'Is this bloke annoying you?' he asked her.

The bride tittered. 'Not yet,' she replied, 'But give it time. We've only been married a few hours!'

Thankfully she left it at that, not allowing Roy an opportunity to apologise, but also sparing his blushes.

At about midnight we were on the verge of leaving when the band came on again for a final hurrah. They fulfilled their promise to the bride to the letter, playing traditional Irish music for about 90 minutes. Roy, who often does pub gigs himself, regretted not having his banjo with him. Given the toll the Guinness had taken on him by then it was probably just as well. When we finally got to bed it was gone two.

For the one and only time in our lives we arrived slightly late at the cricket. However, we were in time to see the first wicket of the day, Daryll Cullinan caught by Ramprakash off Angus Fraser for 56. From then on it was a bit of a procession and South Africa were all out for just 208. England then made a convincing start to their second innings.

That evening, our last at the campsite, we did not follow the hair of the dog doctrine, but instead had a relatively sober night. We didn't have tickets for the following day, but with England needing just 139 to win with nine wickets in hand we slept soundly. In the event they only lost one more wicket and ran out comfortable winners by eight wickets.

* * *

By the next time we wanted to visit Trent Bridge the hotel had closed their little camping area and so we were on the lookout for another campsite. I found one less than five miles from the ground that seemed ideal and made a booking.

I was the first to arrive, but Roy was just a few minutes behind me. Once he arrived we approached reception, but long before we got that far we were accosted by two women in their 60s who asked us to state our business. I said who we were but was immediately told by one of them to wait there while she checked her bookings. As she disappeared in the direction of her house her co-conspirator began to acquaint us with the rules. Firstly, no dogs, no children and no visitors. I had intended to invite the England team over for a post-match beer, but they would probably have declined. Reluctantly, I surrendered this aspiration. So far, so good.

There followed a list as long as your arm of all the things that were not permitted ending with the news that the front gates would be locked at 10pm. As Roy and I reeled from the rules and curfews, her pal reappeared with a hard-backed notepad. Reluctantly she conceded that we were booked in.

Roy and I looked at each other.

'Thank you for your hospitable welcome, but I think we will look elsewhere,' Roy exclaimed. 'Goodnight!'

They looked amazed although I found it hard to believe that we were the first to react in this way.

As we walked away I looked at my watch. It was already 6.30pm and we had nowhere to stay.

'Don't fret, we'll find somewhere,' said Roy in reply to my unspoken question. 'I passed a pub on the way in who had a couple of caravans in the car park. We'll try them.'

Roy climbed into his VW camper van, which he affectionately refers to as 'Dorothy', and started her up, the distinctive sound of the flat engine reminding me immediately of the many Beetles I have owned. He set off in the direction in which he had come and I followed in my car. After no more than five minutes he pulled into a pub car park where, as well as a number of older cars, three sorry-looking caravans had taken up residence. From each caravan a long orange cable went across the car park and down through the beer drop hatch into the cellar.

'Those caravans look permanent to me,' I said as we both parked our vehicles. 'I don't know how they'll feel about putting us up for just a few nights.'

'There's one way to find out,' Roy replied, and locking Dorothy headed for the pub door.

Roy pushed against the rough crumbling paintwork of the door. The hinges squealed as if warning us, but the sound was at once silenced by a wall of noise. There was a stagnant stench of old cigarettes blending with the smell of beer and a hint of vomit and disinfectant.

If this pub had been my idea Roy would have given me one of his disdainful big brother looks and turned for the door, but it was his suggestion.

'This'll do us,' he announced. 'I wonder which one is the landlord?'

'Well, there are about 40 pissed blokes in here and one woman behind the bar. Perhaps we should start with her.'

I remained near the door anticipating a rejection while Roy strode up to the barmaid/landlady and stated his business. Three minutes later he returned with two pints and the news that we were booked in for £10 a night, £12 if we wanted electricity. He seemed pleased with himself.

From across the room a portly man with old egg stains on his jumper was giving us a thumbs-up and smiling. I sort of smiled back. Roy raised his hand in a warm greeting.

'That's the landlord, Jim. Seems a nice bloke.'

I finally took a slug of my beer and was surprised and relieved to discover that, although Jim appeared a rather slovenly fellow, this did not apply to the way in which he kept his ale. It was excellent. Resistance was futile. We were staying.

The following morning, we got up at about eight and looked around for the toilet. There wasn't one. Finding somewhere to have a pee wasn't too much of a problem, but we knew that sooner or later our need for a loo would become more urgent. I went to the pub door and knocked. I knocked again, no answer. I backed away from the door and called Jim's name, after all we were pals now.

Nothing happened for a minute or so and then above us a sash window was raised in one of the bedrooms. Jim rested his ample paunch on the windowsill and peered out.

'We were wondering where the loo is,' I said cheerily.

'You need to use the pub toilet.'

'Everywhere's locked,' I informed him rather unnecessarily.

'You can use it when I open up,' Jim told me.

'How long will that be?'

'We open at half eleven.' Jim pulled his belly in, shut the window and presumably went back to bed.

* * *

In 2001 we had tickets for the last three days of the fourth Ashes Test at Headingley. During England's long barren run in Ashes fixtures stretching from 1987 to the iconic victory in 2005, one became used to turning up for matches with the series already decided. That was again the case this time with England going into the Test already 3-0 down. I had unfortunately been at the first Test, which England lost by an innings and 118 runs.

As usual I was trying to be optimistic. Over the previous three Tests Australia's margin of victory was at least reducing. In this match Australia had posted over 400 in their first innings for the third time that summer, but England had come back strongly on day two, reaching 155/2 by the close. This could be our match.

We had found a campsite about ten miles from the ground and had set up camp by five in the afternoon on the Friday. The woman that owned the site was particularly friendly and so we decided to consult her regarding a pub where we could eat and have a few pints.

'That's an easy one,' she told us. 'There's a great pub a short walk from here that does food and sells excellent beer. You exit the site that way,' she said pointing, 'turn left and walk alongside the old railway track until you reach it. I usually go there on a Friday so I might see you.'

'I think that settles it,' I said to Roy and about two hours later we set off.

It was a pleasant walk on an August evening and, given we were in animated conversation about the prospects for the following day's play, we seemed to arrive soon enough. It was, as we had been told, a cracking pub. The site owner gave us a wave and a smile but did not come over. She was on her own as far as I could make out but seemed to know just about everyone and was the life and soul of the place.

Walking home that night we realised that the walk along the disused railway was longer than we had imagined. It was made worse by the fact there was no moon whatsoever and we found ourselves stumbling along by the light of our mobile phones.

On Saturday morning we woke up at about seven. As usual Roy was the first one out of bed and soon he set about making a cup of tea. We were usually in Roy's camper van and it fell to him to bring all the essentials with him, i.e. milk, bread, eggs, tea, coffee, cereal, etc. This may sound unfair, but he keeps his van stocked up with most of these items anyway, so it was no big deal for him to carry this responsibility. I am slightly ashamed to say that I had never shown either gratitude or interest in what he provides until this particular day when he announced he had forgotten the tea bags.

'What? Of all things you've forgotten the tea?'

To me this was synonymous with leaving the tickets at home.

'What are we going to do?'

By 'we' I really meant 'you' and Roy certainly interpreted it that way. He was proud of his flawless record in these matters and took his own failure to heart.

'I'll go and ask at one of the caravans,' he suggested. 'They're bound to have a few tea bags to spare.'

He looked over to our left where a fat bloke in a string vest was just starting on his first can of lager. However, on the other side of us was a chap in khaki shorts and a white shirt. As Roy looked over to him he gave us a cheery wave. Roy rewarded the man's bonhomie with a winning smile and headed over to his pitch.

Five minutes later he returned clutching two tea bags. He held them up for my approval, two individually wrapped bags of Pukka wild apple tea. Roy had a wistful expression on his face.

'He said if we didn't like them he had some crushed pineapple,' he informed me.

Reluctantly we opted for coffee.

Eventually we recovered from the tea trauma and watched a good day's cricket with England making 309 all out.

However, by the end of play Australia were 207 ahead with nine wickets still in hand. It looked like we would be chasing a challenging total.

That evening we set off again for the pub along the railway track and spent another good night there. Our site owner was there again, but this time she did come over to talk to us just before we left.

'Just letting you boys know that this pub doesn't serve food on a Sunday evening so if you are planning on coming down again you need to eat first.'

We thanked her for her kindness in letting us know and set off back. It really was a hell of a trek.

Sunday was an interesting day, although weather-affected, and before the close Australian captain Adam Gilchrist surprised some by declaring, leaving England a target of 315 with slightly more than a day to bat. It was in many ways a statement of how dominant the Australian team felt with regard to England and I don't think Gilchrist had even the slightest concern about England reaching such a total on the last day.

Roy and I talked about it all the way back to the site and completely forgot the owner's warning that there would be no food available.

Back at the site we suddenly remembered.

'Sod it, I'm bloody starving already,' Roy admitted.

Just at that moment another camper emerged from his caravan. The state of his awning told us that he probably had a seasonal pitch. I called across to him and he walked over. We exchanged pleasantries and finally I asked him where we might eat that evening.

'Go out of the site on to the railway track, turn right and there's a pub about two hundred yards along. They serve food on a Sunday.'

Roy and I looked bemused. I was the first to speak.

'We've been walking about four miles every night to a pub down the hill from there. The woman who runs this site recommended it. She never mentioned there was one only five minutes away!'

Our new pal smiled to himself.

'Well that's no mystery,' he said with a chuckle. 'She doesn't only own the site, she owns the pub as well!'

The following day at the cricket was one of those you dream of being at. Roy and I both had a high opinion of Mark Butcher, both as a batsman and as an all-rounder, but his performance on that last day went beyond any of our expectations. Butcher recorded his highest ever Test score, carrying his bat on 173 not out and leading England to a momentous victory. Although supported by Nasser Hussain and later Mark Ramprakash it was largely a one-man performance. At all times Butcher was not only aware of the target score he was also keeping up with the required scoring rate, his 173 coming off just 227 deliveries. Despite being hoodwinked by our host we went home happy.

* * *

Our most intriguing experience of all was also in Yorkshire. It was early in 2004 and we were there to watch England versus New Zealand at Headingley. We had tickets for days two, three and four, Friday to Sunday.

We had booked into a campsite that we had never used before and had agreed to make an early start and meet at the campsite before the start of play. We both arrived with little time to spare, parked Roy's camper van at the site and headed towards the ground. We would erect the awning later. We were there long enough to take note of the beautiful scenery and on the way out of the village noticed a very inviting-looking pub no more than 400 yards from the site. So far, so good.

England had put New Zealand in to bat the morning before on a damp, overcast day. However, due to rain and bad light, there had been only just over an hour's play with New Zealand finishing on 41/1. Now on a bright morning they were probably glad to have lost the toss. As it turned out they finished day two well placed on 351/6.

Roy and I drove back to the campsite, put up the awning and had a quick shower. By 8pm we were ready to check out the local pub. And what a find it turned out to be.

The pub sold excellent food including a decent choice for vegetarians and more importantly excellent ale. Their session beer was Tetley's bitter and in addition they had three or four guest ales. The landlord, who turned out to be a cricket nut, made us very welcome. Once he found out that we were in Yorkshire for the Test match he announced the fact to the whole pub.

It is not unusual to go to pubs in Yorkshire and find a clientele who are very knowledgeable about the game and this was the case here. However, the landlord was not predisposed to give his regulars an easy time. He and a friend had tickets for the Saturday which allowed him to give the locals a dressing down as he introduced us.

'See, these lads are not armchair fans like you lot. They've travelled miles to support their team and good on 'em, I say.'

With that he declared that our first drink was on the house!

When Roy and I are out for the night we like to have a few pints before we eat. For that reason we are always fairly eager to find out when the kitchen is due to close. I put this question to one of the lads with whom we were sitting. He looked at me quizzically, appearing not to understand the question.

'If he's open he's serving,' was his simple reply. I must admit I have often wondered why so many establishments who are in business to serve food and drink stop doing meals quite early in the evening. However, we have been caught out too many times so when I next went to the bar I put the same question to the landlord.

'When you lads want to eat, just let me know,' he said.

This was getting too good to be true.

We spent a really enjoyable evening at the pub soaking up the atmosphere. We eventually returned to the campsite at about 11pm. As is his custom, Roy produced a bottle of whiskey, and we spent a pleasant half hour reflecting on how lucky we were while Roy celebrated his infinite wisdom in finding the site in the first place.

We woke at about seven to a glorious day and sat outside drinking tea just taking in the scene. Seeing us at this time of day you would think we were on different continents. Roy sits there with about six layers of clothing on and a cap whereas I usually wear just a T-shirt!

It really was a picturesque campsite, but with one quirky feature. We had become accustomed to recycling arrangements at almost all campsites and had been surprised to be told to simply empty our rubbish on a large tip on the edge of the site. As we sat sipping our tea the campsite owner appeared and with the help of copious amounts of paraffin set light to the rubbish tip. We had wondered what would be done with the accumulated refuse, but we had not anticipated this particular solution.

Having assured himself that the blaze was safely contained the owner wished us a cheery good morning and went back into his office. Roy and I looked at each other blankly, astonished at what we had witnessed. However, knowing that the need to 'do something' would be gnawing away at me, Roy authoritatively proclaimed it as 'their business'.

'We've got a very interesting Test match to attend and the chance of a few more pints later on,' he declared and with that the subject was closed.

At the match, Chris Cairns was out almost as soon as we arrived and after a quickfire 50 from Brendon McCullum New Zealand lost their last three wickets without adding to the score. Nevertheless, 409 was a very decent total for a team who had been put into bat. England went in pursuit of New Zealand's score like a steam train with Marcus Trescothick clocking up 132 in quick time. England were going at almost four an over, a precursor for how they would bat in the Ashes a year later. At close they were 248/4. Roy and I returned to the campsite well satisfied with an exciting day of top cricket.

Our visit to the pub that night was almost a repeat performance of the previous evening, but with the addition of an excited landlord regaling his customers with the events of the day. We had another fabulous evening and left promising everyone we would be back on Sunday for our final night.

We enjoyed an incredible day's cricket during which England completely turned the game around. England completed their first innings, reaching a staggering 526 in which Flintoff scored 94 and the wicketkeeper Geraint Jones reached exactly 100 in just 146 balls. In a helter-skelter day England then went on to take five New Zealand wickets for just 102. The game was all but over, and we went back to the campsite in the secure knowledge that England would wrap things up the following morning.

After a swift shower we were on our way to the best cricketing pub we had ever been to. However, a nasty surprise was waiting for us. It was quiz night. We both hate quizzes, mainly because we are rubbish at them. We are both okay on politics or literature, about which you might get one or two questions, and not bad on most mainstream sports, but on any other subject we are hopeless. In particular we are of no use on trivia or TV, films or any questions about celebrities. We also know that sitting separately trying to chat is virtually impossible.

We stood on the threshold wondering what to do although in reality there was no other choice. As we entered hesitantly we were immediately approached by various locals trying everything to sign us up for their team. We tried to insist they would be making a big error, but in the end we had to grin and bear it. We joined a team which without us consisted of just two brothers, but they were nice folk who seemed glad to have us.

The quiz was in two halves with sandwiches in the interval. At the halfway point we were placed second from last. Roy had answered one question about the novelist, William Thackeray, and I found myself able to identify two songs sung by Kenny Lynch.

As the second half began the landlord had a twinkle in his eye as he prepared to ask the first question. It was an easy one about Ian Botham that most people knew, but we were the only people in the pub unaware that the whole of the second half was to consist of cricket questions. With Roy knowing every single historical question and me mopping up the contemporary ones, we swept the board.

Our team-mates were delighted and immediately headed to the bar to refill our glasses. I don't know whether there was a cash prize or if everyone was just very generous, but we didn't buy a drink the whole night.

Eventually we said our goodbyes and walked back to our camper van with a warm glow.

Two years later we were planning to go to Headingley to watch England play Pakistan and we were keen to return to the same campsite with the wonderful pub just up the road. Try as we may we could not identify it, nor could we recall the name of the pub or the village. We have tried many times since and never been successful. In his famous essay in the *Evening Standard* on 9 February 1946 George Orwell describes his favourite public house, the Moon Under Water, in considerable detail. He talks of the excellence of the lunches, the fine quality of the beer and the friendliness of the locals. However, the thing that appeals to him most about the Moon Under Water is its 'atmosphere'. The irony is that the Moon Under Water does not actually exist. Roy and I often wonder if we imagined the whole thing.

Chapter 15

Cricket, Sri Lanka and Me

THROUGHOUT THE 1980s and early 90s I watched a lot of cricket with my great friend Ewen. His dad, as I have said previously, was an ex-professional cricketer who usually acquired the tickets for us. Somewhere along the line Ewen went to live abroad. I saw him for a brief spell in the mid-90s when he came back to the UK for a short while, but for a long time after that we pretty well lost touch.

This was entirely my fault as he used to write quite often and, although I always intended to, I rarely wrote back. Twenty years passed and then in 2012 he phoned me out of the blue. I did not know at the time that he had phoned me on his birthday. Apparently he had decided on this as a birthday present to himself. Suddenly all the reasons why we got on so well were there to be seen and I was at first racked with guilt that I had been so poor at keeping in touch. Ewen was not interested in this. He wanted to hear about my life and tell me something about his. The phone conversation was ridiculously easy and we both followed up with emails bringing each other up to date.

Ewen and his wife Pauline had always had a 'rather lively' relationship and I was sad, but not surprised, to learn that they were divorced. After stints working in Saudi Arabia and Oman he had settled in Kandy, Sri Lanka with his Sri Lankan wife Padma who he loved to bits. He was working for the British Council teaching English and as he was now approaching 60 had reduced his workload to three days per week.

Only a few weeks after speaking to him he and Padma came to the UK to visit Ewen's parents in Northants. I took the opportunity to go down to see him there which was brilliant and I was also able to meet his lovely wife. Both of them seemed really happy living in Kandy and each of them implored me to visit them there. By way of encouragement Ewen reminded me that Kandy was a Test match venue. I was tempted, but Marieluise and I were in the early stages of considering a move to Bulgaria, so it was not really feasible at the time. However, it was certainly something I wanted to consider in the future.

Shortly afterwards they returned to Sri Lanka and we kept loosely in touch, mainly by email. Marieluise and I did move to Bulgaria and in the summer of 2014 I got in touch with him. I had been thinking about him that day and without warning I made a video call via Skype. When I got through to him he could hear me okay, but said the picture was blurred.

'I'll move to another room where the internet signal is stronger,' he suggested and did just that.

'Oh my God, how awful,' he exclaimed two minutes later. I could see his face screwing up.

'What's up?' I asked slightly bewildered.

'Nothing, it's just that I can see you now!' The sort of ironic reply I knew so well.

'I got in touch because you keep saying I should come to Sri Lanka and I wanted you to know that I have moved to Bulgaria so I am now halfway there!'

Ewen feigned pleasure. I continued in this knockabout vein until he suddenly told me that Padma had terminal cancer. I just went quiet at first as he filled the silence with more background information. It was devastating news, but he told me all about it with such immense courage.

Padma died later that year. I am glad to say that Ewen had some good friends around him in Kandy who helped him through it. There was also his poetry. We had both written poetry for a number of years, but suddenly his poems about loss took his writing to a new level. I think it helped him a lot.

During Padma's illness Ewen's son, Ben, had been in contact with his dad almost every day. It was therefore great news for Ewen when sometime later Ben got a job in Kandy and moved there with his Chinese wife, Lin. I had not seen Ben since he was about eight or nine and so if I did finally get round to visiting Kandy I would have the added pleasure of meeting Ben again, now in his mid-30s.

From that point on we kept properly in touch and Ewen came to see us in Wales at Christmas 2017. By then I had run out of excuses for not visiting him in Sri Lanka and in 2018 England were due to tour there. The second Test was pencilled in to be played in Kandy. I was ready to roll.

I arrived at Colombo Airport in the early hours of 10 November 2018 to the news from the previous day that Sri Lanka were all out for 250 in their second innings at Galle, giving England victory in the first Test by 211 runs. We were due to watch the second Test from the following Wednesday.

Although my plane had arrived three hours late, it was just 15 minutes ahead of Ewen. He had been waiting at a nearby guest house watching arrival times on his phone. It was great to finally be in the country that my friend firmly regarded as home. After a late kip and my first ever curried breakfast at the guest house, we set off for Kandy.

Ewen's house is absolutely lovely. It is only 20 minutes from the city, but within walking distance of primary rainforest where I was to discover later you can see wild pigs, porcupines, snakes, wild cats including fruit bats with a 3ft wingspan. You don't have to go into the forest to see monkeys as they visit the house most days.

Kandy itself is especially beautiful. The city sits at an altitude of about 1,600 feet above sea level. Its centre is dominated by a large square, with the administration buildings of the old capital at the end, and an artificial lake. A public garden adds to the sense of openness of the city centre. The buildings are generally quite colourful and the varied styles of architecture reflect the different cultural influences from Kandy's rich history.

On the first full day we took a three-wheeler into town to go for a walk around the lake. Before realising it was the only means of getting about in Kandy, I swore I would never get in a three-wheeler again. The guy drove the tiny unstable vehicle like a lunatic. At one point we squeezed between two buses travelling in the opposite direction to us with only inches to spare on either side. During this short journey the driver spoke incessantly about the forthcoming Test match and how he hoped the Sri Lankan team would turn things around after their heavy defeat at Galle. I have to admit that I did not pick up the details of what he was saying as I just closed my eyes and prayed throughout the whole terrifying episode. I was in the city for at least two hours before I was sure which side of the road they drive on. They seemed to just drive on whichever side offered the opportunity of making progress. The traffic was loud and chaotic.

Once we 'landed' the lake views were breathtaking. We walked slowly, taking it all in and giving ourselves the opportunity to catch up and share news. Ewen and I have always been close despite the long periods of not seeing each other and as usual we fell back into an easy conversation as if we had been together the previous week. It was important to him that I liked the place where he has made his home and he was eager to show Kandy off to its best advantage. He did not have to try very hard as I loved it from the start.

We had a relaxing day and so I was not prepared for the shock when we returned home. It was me who entered the house first while Ewen fiddled with the gate. The kitchen had been ransacked with all the cupboards open and their contents strewn across the floor. Looking into the living room I could see it had not been spared.

'Ewen, you've been burgled!' I called out to him.

As he entered the kitchen he surveyed the devastation surrounding him.

'Did you leave your bedroom window open?' he asked.

'I'm not sure, I might have,' I replied. 'But nobody could have climbed up and got in there,' I added in my defence.

'That may be true, but we have not been burgled by humans. We've had a visit from the monkeys.'

I looked around again, only this time with new eyes. It was immediately clear that the perpetrators had been in search of food. Anything that was not to their liking was discarded indiscriminately. They seemed most interested in sugar, cakes, some vegetables and of course fruit, particularly bananas of which Ewen always had a good supply. Not anymore. There was a trail of banana skins up the stairs into my room where they had clearly both entered and exited. A bookcase had been turned over and the porcelain bedside lamp lay shattered on the ground.

Ewen took the whole thing in his stride, finding amusement in my shock and guilt.

'I can only assume they were hungry,' he remarked with a grin and once we had cleared up the matter was forgotten.

Over the next couple of days we did some more sightseeing including a visit to a wildlife park where I saw a large number of monkeys, although I did not spot any with a guilty look on their face. Maybe our intruders were more local.

Ewen employed a local woman called Seela as a cook and cleaner. She had been a great support during Padma's illness and he was very fond of her. I got the impression that she had quite a difficult domestic life as she often stayed on when there was little to do. She would often relax and just hang out. Ewen seemed more than happy with the arrangement. Seela had a very infectious laugh and it was nice having her around.

Part of her remit was to cook lunch. Staying with Ewen in the past, the catering was never a great highlight, but thanks to Seela all that changed. Each day I was treated to a superb curry made from the simplest ingredients. The key was her use of herbs and spices which was magical.

Our breakfasts usually consisted of muesli, fruit and sometimes yoghurt, but on the day before the cricket Ewen decided to take me into Kandy for a Sri Lankan breakfast. We arrived at a huge open-air eating place with a very long serving area. Behind the counter was a long line of women and in front of them was the food they had for sale.

Ewen explained that each of the women brought their own ingredients, cooked there and laid out their wonderful offerings to the public who came forward and bought whatever took their fancy. He advised me to just buy a few small dishes at a time and then go back for something else. I did as I was told and the variety was infinite. Every dish was very spicy and some were quite hot. I would happily have stayed there all morning.

We remained in town and got caught in a downpour, but there were plenty of cafes and bars in which to take shelter. When the rain stopped we headed out to find a three-wheeler to get us home. The road up to Ewen's house was very steep and given how wet the roads were the three-wheeler could not make it up the hill. It appeared as if Ewen had met this situation before as he simply got out and walked alongside until the road levelled out enough for the vehicle to proceed.

Given all the different things we had done beforehand the first day of the Test almost took me by surprise. Given the lovely weather I had been getting up early so I had time to acclimatise to the idea of watching a Test match. Ewen and I sat having breakfast discussing the prospects for the day's play. Soon it all felt quite familiar.

For a long time touring Sri Lanka had been a formidable prospect for any Test team. They had a number of high-class batsmen including Mahela Jayawardene, Sanath Jayasuriya and the formidable wicketkeeper/batsman Kumar Sangakkara. They also had a world class spinner, Muttiah Muralitharan, who on Sri Lankan pitches could be virtually unplayable. Finally there was their enigmatic fast bowler, Lasith Malinga, known for his distinctive round-arm action resulting in the nickname of 'Slinga Malinga'.

Before this series each one of them had retired and although Sri Lanka were still a decent side playing at home, they had a very inexperienced line-up. England had won the first Test by 211 runs and the expectation was that they would win again.

We set off early for the Pallekele Stadium given that games in Sri Lanka start at 10am and also because the ground is a good 40 minutes from the city. It is a fabulous stadium with the hills in the background. By English standards it is a very large cricket ground with a capacity of

35,000. It is really well designed, affording good views from all round the stadium including from the grass banking where lots of the locals sit and the atmosphere is electric. However, if you sit here you are pretty well in the sun all day and it was seriously hot.

It soon became evident that the Barmy Army were out in force as they were singing and drinking before Ewen and I had finished our first coffee. What lightweights we had become since our prime during the 1981 Botham Ashes!

When we did get round to having a few drinks I discovered that the beer was good and cheap and the service was quick. However, although the beer prices were okay, there had been a lot of dissatisfaction from the Barmy Army prior to the game. At one point the match was in doubt because the Earls Regency Hotel could not accommodate the players due to the large number of bookings they had taken from the Barmy Army. The England fans had no option but to give way so that the players could be accommodated.

Chris Millard, the Army's managing director, said, 'It is inadequate that this has happened for such a series that brings a huge following of people to the country. They have been let down by the [Sri Lanka] Cricket Board.'

The government later booked 69 rooms at three other hotels for the Barmy Army members, but the new hotels were two hours from the ground at Kandy compared to the 15-minute drive from the Earls Regency.

It further emerged that the Barmy Army were being charged £50 per day for their members' tickets whereas the locals were only paying £1.50 to sit on the grass banks! The Barmy Army immediately launched a campaign in protest and soon after the cricket authorities agreed that England fans could access the grass banks at the same price as locals.

When play did get underway, England won the toss and elected to bat. However, things did not go well and at one point they had slumped to 176/7. Partial respectability was restored by some rapid-fire lower-order batting from Adil Rashid and Sam Curran, whose 64 included six sixes. One of the highlights of the day was when a towering Sam Curran six landed amongst the Barmy Army contingent and was superbly caught by one of their members, Richard Nicholls, giving him instant celebrity status. In the end England made only 290, a poor return for a side electing to bat first, and by the close Sri Lanka had reached 26 for the loss of one of their openers, Kaushal Silva.

That evening we went for a drink and something to eat at a beautiful bar where we were able to sit outside on the bank of the Mahaweli River. Ewen's son Ben joined us, on his own as his wife was visiting her parents in China. We had a really nice evening although I did have to cope with the difficult news that Ben preferred football to cricket. He had of course grown up in Liverpool so I guess it was inevitable.

Thursday morning and back to the Pallekele Stadium for day two. A steady performance from the Sri Lanka batsmen saw them reach 336 all out with three players making half-centuries. The best of those came from Roshen Silva, who batted sensibly for 85. He is an undemonstrative batsman, lacking the style of the famous Sri Lankan batsmen of the past, but very effective at accumulating runs. It was largely thanks to Silva that Sri Lanka accrued a very handy first innings lead. With the exception of the run-out of Dimuth Karunaratne, the left-handed opener, every wicket was taken by an England spinner, not something either of us had ever experienced, certainly not in a first innings. The seamers bowled only 19 overs between them.

This left time for just one over and we witnessed the unusual sight of the England No.10 Jack Leach opening the batting. He did his job and England ended the day on nought with all ten wickets intact. Nevertheless, they were 46 runs behind on first innings.

Unusually we took a conventional taxi back to Ewen's rather than a three-wheeler so we could discuss the day's play without having to compete with the sound of the engine. Our general conclusion was that the match was fairly evenly poised, although with Sri Lanka having to bat last England possibly had a slight advantage.

We had planned to go into town that evening, but Ewen was feeling a bit under the weather so we decided to spend an evening at home. As the evening wore on Ewen started to feel increasingly unwell. He was feeling lethargic with a bad headache and aching muscles. Later still he developed a temperature at which point we both decided he needed to see a doctor.

It was now about 9pm so we ordered a three-wheeler and asked him to take us to A&E.

The arrangements at A&E at first sight seemed chaotic with a huge gaggle of people standing in a large clump hoping for attention. However, there was a system. Facing the potential patients from behind a desk was a doctor and a nurse with a consulting room behind them. They called people forward in turn to assess their problem although how they determined who was next was a mystery to me. After a brief interview each person was either taken into the consulting room or sent on their way.

In our case we had only been waiting about ten minutes when we were called forward. There was no way it was our turn and Ewen had certainly done nothing to suggest he should be given priority. In the end there was only one explanation. We were being given priority because we were white. After a lot of thought and discussion with people who know the country well my conclusion was that colonial legacies continue to govern Sri Lankans' sense of identity and society. They see themselves as law-abiding people and rate each other according to how hard-working they are in their service to the dominant colonial culture. It is virtually a self-imposed racism.

In the end the hospital could do nothing for us as they did not have the facilities required to undertake a blood test that would likely determine what was wrong with Ewen. It was now quite late and the advice was to go home, drink plenty of fluids and return in the morning. Reluctantly we did as we had been advised.

The following morning Ewen's high temperature was unabated, and he was starting to show signs of delirium. Ewen is prone to talking nonsense, especially in my company, but it usually occurs when he is under the influence of alcohol. On this occasion I was forced to conclude that the delusions and incoherence he was displaying were as a result of fever. I ordered a three-wheeler and Ewen mustered enough sense to tell the guy to take him to a different hospital where he had previously been an inpatient.

Once we arrived Ewen was seen immediately and it did not take long to establish that he had dengue fever. He was immediately admitted to an isolation ward and I was told to go home.

I wandered outside feeling worried and uncertain. I decided that in the first instance I would find a cafe, order a strong coffee and try to get my head straight.

It suddenly occurred to me that Ewen's son, Ben, knew nothing about his dad's hospitalisation. I had his number in my phone and gave him a call. Unfortunately, he did not answer. I assumed he was probably teaching and resolved to ring him again in an hour or so. I decided to hail a three-wheeler and go back to Ewen's house. Seela obviously needed to be told what was going on and anyway her lunches were better than I was likely to get in town. There is no point starving just because your best mate has dengue fever. I needed to stay strong.

Sitting in the three-wheeler, the driver asked the obvious question.

'Where to, sir?'

For the first time I realised that I did not know Ewen's address. Somewhere in the past I had needed it in order to get a visa, but I had since completely forgotten it, even the name of the district.

'I'm not sure of the address, but I think I can find it,' I told the driver and immediately I started giving directions.

I began explaining to the guy what had happened, but he didn't seem interested. If some weird Englishman wanted to drive aimlessly around Kandy that was fine by him as long as he paid the fare.

For ten minutes or so I was doing well, but 20 minutes after we had left town I had to admit I was hopelessly lost. I tried Ben again and this time, thank heaven, he answered.

I explained everything that had happened and finally got round to telling him about my current difficulty of not being able to find the house. I was that worked up I think Ben believed I had a fever too! He made the very practical suggestion that I hand my phone to the driver.

After a brief conversation the driver returned my phone and set off with more purpose. It soon became evident that I had not been completely off beam as five minutes later we pulled up outside Ewen's house. Although he picked up a decent fare and a generous tip I got the distinct impression that the driver was glad to see the back of me. He took my money and drove off at speed without a backward glance.

Seela had prepared a delicious dhal curry which she told me was Ewen's favourite meal. The dhal is boiled with turmeric which gives the dish that lovely orangey colour and also enhances the flavour. She was very concerned to hear that he had dengue fever and, as she told me about some of her relatives who had dengue and did not survive, my alarm increased considerably.

After Seela went home I phoned Ben again, wanting to apologise for being such a plonker and to see if he was okay after my shock news about his dad. He was less troubled than me and told me that the worst symptoms of the illness typically last one to two weeks, and that most patients fully recover. It is apparently fatal in less than one per cent of cases.

'Try not to worry,' he told me.

Somehow I could not avoid the feeling that this conversation should have been the other way round. Ewen had told me how calm and measured Ben was, and here I could see it being played out in practice.

It was a beautiful day and after a shower I made myself a cup of tea, cut a slice of cake and went outside to read. Meanwhile Joe Root, unaware that one of his biggest fans lay seriously ill in hospital and a second who had come 6,000 miles to see him was missing in action, reached his century at almost a run a ball. Even without us there to cheer him on he had turned the match decidedly in England's favour. Sri Lanka would need 301 to win.

On Saturday, 17 November (day four) as Sri Lanka set about an unlikely run chase, I went with Ben to visit his dad. We arrived to the unwelcome news that he had been transferred to intensive care 'as a precaution'. The next time I heard that someone was being admitted to intensive care 'as a precaution' it was Prime Minister Boris Johnson. I was certain that people only went into an ITU because they needed the intensive care on offer so I did not believe the explanation on either occasion.

A doctor who was not caring for Ewen during this illness, but knew him from a previous admission, told me casually that for many years they had been over-hydrating patients with dengue fever. As a result they had apparently lost more patients than they otherwise would have.

'We've got the balance just right now,' he continued. 'Your friend will be fine.'

By Sunday lunchtime England had won the Test match by 57 runs, again with all the Sri Lankan wickets falling to spinners, and Ewen's recovery had begun. That evening I went for a pint with Ben and a group of friends who were also friends of his father. Everyone was relieved that Ewen was suddenly much better.

On Tuesday I was due to fly home, and it was clear that my friend would remain in hospital until after I had left. Now that he knew his dad would be alright Ben was determined that I would get something from my remaining couple of days in Sri Lanka and he happily took over the role of host. He asked me what I had hoped to see and I told him that we had planned to go to an elephant sanctuary. The next morning I visited Ewen to say goodbye and an hour later Ben and I were on our way.

I had a great final day. The elephant sanctuary was amazing. I also found time to buy some presents for the family; in particular I was able to buy Sri Lanka cricket shirts for my grandchildren.

That evening we stayed at a guest house in Negombo, a lovely beach town located about an hour away from Colombo airport. Ben took me to a well-known seafood restaurant. There he tried to encourage me to put my feet into a tank containing tiny flesh-eating fish. Most customers seemed happy to indulge in this ritual which Ben assured me was very pleasant. However, I could not be convinced and like a proper England cricket fan abroad I decided to keep my socks on.

The following morning we got the news that Ewen was due to be discharged from hospital later that day, which allowed me to feel more settled for my homeward journey. Ben drove me to the airport and soon I was on my way home. I sat on the plane and reflected on a strange ten days. As with the England cricket team I had started well. England had won the toss and I had seen a lot of the beautiful city of Kandy and enjoyed two good days of cricket with one of my closest friends. Like England, who won the match, I had finished well, spending two memorable days with Ewen's son who I only remembered as a young child. Unfortunately for me things had gone rather awry in the middle overs.

Chapter 16

Our World Cup Year

THE 2019 World Cup was the 12th staged, but although England had often got close and had hosted the competition on four previous occasions, they had never won it. However, this time England started out as the No.1 ranked international one-day team. Hopes were high. The tournament took place between 30 May and 14 July across 11 venues in England and Wales.

The finals of this World Cup were contested by ten teams, a decrease from 14 teams in the previous event four years earlier, with the format changing to a single round-robin group with the top four teams qualifying through to the knockout stage.

Very early on the competition touched our family much more closely than we could ever have expected. Emily's two children, Finlay and Iris, play junior cricket for our local club Carmel and the club had been chosen to provide the mascots for the first game to be played in Wales at Sophia Gardens in Cardiff.

In an attempt to create an ongoing cricket legacy in the family I had introduced Fin and Iris to the game at the ages of seven and five respectively. For two seasons I took them to evening training at a small village club near our home, Halkyn CC. The standard of training was good, but right from the start Halkyn struggled with numbers in the junior set-up and when they did get the opportunity to play an under-9s match they had to borrow heavily from the opposition in order to put out a team.

In the second season the numbers fell further. I had worked hard to instil the concept of team loyalty in both of them so when I decided we should seek another club it was Fin and Iris who resisted. The president of the Halkyn club, Robin, is a good friend of mine and it was only when I told the youngsters that we had his blessing if we wanted to move on that they relented. On Robin's advice Iris and Fin joined Carmel CC where they now enjoy training and get regular opportunities to play in competitive matches. Given how early they started they have both become good cricketers with Fin often playing above his age group.

Finlay and Iris were only in their second season with Carmel when, along with their team-mates, they struck gold and were chosen to be mascots for the New Zealand team to play Sri Lanka.

On 1 June 2019 the junior cricketers from Carmel set off by coach very early as they needed to be at the ground two hours before the scheduled start of the match in order to 'rehearse' their roles as mascots. Iris and Finlay were accompanied by their dad, Andrew and their grandad, me. It is difficult to say who was more excited, the kids or us.

The preparation once we got to the ground was mightily impressive and when the time came they were all well drilled in their roles. Iris was mascot to wicketkeeper/batsman, Tom Latham and Finlay to opening batsman, Martin Guptill. The players were great with them, asking them about their club and their own cricket exploits. As if to emphasise the point I made earlier about loyalty, Iris told Tom Latham that she played for Halkyn! Fin was later very proud when Guptill top scored with 73 not out as New Zealand reached the target of 137 runs without the loss of a single wicket. Finlay claimed that as his official mascot he was partially responsible for Guptill's good fortune.

The junior players from Carmel were treated like young celebrities, each receiving a World Cup shirt and cap and being given lunch.

After their lunch they played some exhibition cricket in front of an appreciative crowd. They were so pleased with themselves and Andrew and I, not to mention everybody back home, were as proud as Punch.

Fin continued throughout the competition to show an interest in the performances of New Zealand and Martin Guptill in particular, never dreaming they would end up as England's opponents in the final.

* * *

The reader would have realised by now that Roy and I are first and foremost lovers of the longer form of the game, although we have often enjoyed one-day matches.

We were at Trent Bridge in June 2018 when England broke their own world record for the highest ever score in a one-day international, scoring 481/6 as they beat Australia by 242 runs. That was some match. At one point it was so fast and furious we went outside the ground and sat on the kerb for ten minutes, trying to regain our equilibrium.

It was a far cry from the one-day cricket we were brought up on. The wonderful John Player League was broadcast live on the BBC every Sunday afternoon throughout the summer from 1969 until the mid-1980s, Richie Benaud and Jim Laker providing the very unhurried commentary. The 17 first-class counties played each other in a league format every Sunday throughout the season. Unlike modern one-day cricket, any score above about 170 was likely to secure victory.

Except for the fact that a result was achieved in one day, the cricket did not differ greatly in pace and intensity from the normal three-day county game. The players wore normal cricket whites and a red ball was used. It was the perfect fare after a few pints and Sunday lunch.

One-day cricket has since evolved at a rapid rate and modern one-day internationals (ODIs) are now spectacular events. The games are accompanied by a high level of razzmatazz, but it is still the cricket that provides the spectacle. We had not managed to secure any tickets for England World Cup matches, but we followed each one avidly on TV and radio, usually catching up by phone at the end of each day.

England got off to a flyer against South Africa, winning by a big margin, but then immediately tripped up against Pakistan, losing by 14 runs. From that point on they were always slightly up against it as the other three well fancied teams, India, Australia and New Zealand, each got on to a consistent run. Two more defeats meant that England needed to beat India, New Zealand and Australia in consecutive matches to reach the final. This was an incredibly tall order, but finally they discovered the form that had taken them to the top of the world rankings and won all three games.

For Roy and me their total demolition of Australia in the semi-final was particularly satisfying. Australia were bowled out inside the 50 overs and England needed only 32 overs to pass Australia's score with the loss of just two wickets. In common with all England fans we ardently hoped they would take this scintillating run of form into the final.

Roy and I tend to pick out the games at Trent Bridge that we want to see at the start of the season. We then book the campsite for each of these matches and largely stick to our initial plans.

It turned out that on 14 July, the day of the World Cup Final, we were watching the second day of Nottinghamshire versus Surrey. For Notts fans it was not very watchable as by lunchtime on day two our team was already facing certain defeat. Given the state of the match we had come to see, our focus was slowly shifting to the main event, the World Cup Final at Lord's. We weren't the only ones. Stuart Broad was fielding on the boundary right in front of us. Once he discovered that Roy had the final on his phone he kept asking for updates, groaning each time England lost a wicket in their pursuit of New Zealand's modest total of 241.

As the match proceeded to what was clearly going to be a tight finish we joined other fans in the Parr bar clustered around the TV. With 15 overs to go England were still well short on 137/4, but Jos Buttler and Ben Stokes were looking good, trying to bat carefully whilst also attempting to increase the pace. It was time to make a decision. Unfortunately, Notts were giving us little cause for hope and so we agreed to leave the ground in favour of the Trent Bridge Inn with its fine ales and big screen. Watching the World Cup Final in the Trent Bridge Inn with its long cricketing tradition seemed more than appropriate. We felt sure that the pub's 19th-century landlord William Clarke, the original curator of the Trent Bridge cricket ground, would have approved.

The huge room at the back of the Inn that butts on to the cricket ground was heaving. Almost everyone was standing, not through a lack of seats, but because the tension was somehow more bearable in an upright position.

Most people believed that if Stokes and Buttler could stay together then England would reach the target, although by the time we reached the 45th over of the allocated 50 the required run rate had risen to more than nine an over. With the fifth ball of the over disaster struck as Buttler holed out to Tim Southee, the sub, at deep cover from a slower ball from Lockie Ferguson. The room fell silent but eventually the optimists in the crowd started to assert that Stokes could handle it and belief in a successful outcome was re-established.

Next to me a young man was biting his nails with an unhealthy intensity. His girlfriend was seated at the table alongside and, although she clearly knew nothing about cricket, was doing her best to reassure him. I made sure that I stood firmly between the young lad and Roy as it was clear to me that my brother's legendary fatalism would be the last straw for him. He must have asked me 20 times if I thought we would win and each time I told him we would, although I could see that I might be building him up for a very heavy fall.

When the innings were tied and the announcement came that there would be a super over to decide the match I headed for the bar to refresh our glasses. While I was gone the rules of the super over appeared on the screen, but neither Roy nor the young guy next to me had been paying attention. When wicketkeeper Jos Buttler ran out Martin Guptill on the last ball of the match as he dived for the line in vain, we only knew that England had won through the joyous celebrations of Buttler, who went on a spontaneous victory dance. The place erupted and the young man threw his arms around me in a state of complete elation of a sort that only sports fans ever experience.

'I would never have believed that supporting England would bring me such pleasure,' he announced.

Roy gave him a knowing look. 'Good luck with the next 40 years, mate!' was all he said.

Fortunately our new friend was oblivious to the meaning of Roy's words.

Watching on TV with his family back in North Wales, Fin's allegiance to Martin Guptill had been unceremoniously ditched. The player's previously loyal mascot deserted him in his moment of need and yelled with delight as Guptill, sliding on his belly, looked despairingly at the broken stumps. He was still a metre from the line, losing the World Cup 'by the barest of margins'.

That evening Roy and I celebrated long and hard at the Trent Bridge Inn. I remember waking up at the campsite in Stragglethorpe the following morning not entirely sure how or when we arrived there from the pub, but I hardly cared. If I had woken up in a bush it would not have dampened my feelings of elation.

Aged 15 I had watched the England football team win the World Cup standing on a street in Southampton outside a TV shop! In 2003 I had to listen on the radio as the England rugby team won the World Cup with that last-minute Jonny Wilkinson drop goal although Ian Robertson's iconic radio commentary made the moment come alive. Now at last I had been able to watch a World Cup victory in just about the perfect venue. There is probably no pub or bar in the world with such a deep and historic connection with the game of cricket as the Trent Bridge Inn. Watching together with my cricket-mad brother and a host of other cricket fans made it truly special.

Chapter 17

The Barmy Army, My Brother and Me

THE NAME 'Barmy Army', now virtually a British institution, was first conjured up by the Australian media during the 1994/95 Test series in Australia. The press could not quite get their heads round the fans' misguided loyalty in travelling all the way to Australia in the near-certain knowledge that their team would lose and lose badly. As a people who are only really interested in winning, Australians also found it hard to fathom that the England fans kept on chanting encouragement even when their team was losing heavily.

As the caravan of fans arrived at the Adelaide Oval for the fourth Test England were already 2-0 down, but their support for their team was undiminished. The name 'Barmy Army' had stuck and a small group of England fans decided to visit 'T-Shirt City' in Adelaide and order 50 shirts bearing the logo 'Atherton's Barmy Army' with a Union Jack printed on the back. By the end of the match over 200 shirts had been purchased and the small group of fans that had come up with the idea, David Peacock, Paul Burnham and Gareth Evans, realised they were on to something. This was the catalyst for the formal establishment of the Barmy Army. It is worth noting that England won this particular Test but went down 3-1 in the series.

By the end of the series in excess of 8,000 items of merchandise had been sold and the proceeds were spent on trademarking the name Barmy Army in both Australia and England. In March 1995 the company 'Barmy Army Limited' was formed.

Given the circumstances in which Roy and I first encountered the Barmy Army in 1995 it is not surprising that our initial view of them was not entirely positive. Having said that, it was difficult at that time to establish exactly who the Barmy Army was. There had been a lot of publicity about them following their antics in Australia during the recent tour and some cricket supporters were identifying with them, although quite a number were not. The Test grounds did not help the Barmy Army to establish itself, refusing to allow them to make block bookings for matches. In short, the cricket establishment were not wanting to encourage this new type of fan. Nevertheless, a contingent of England fans were offering the type of vocal support the Barmy Army had provided in Australia and in 1995 we found ourselves sitting amongst them.

We were at Old Trafford watching the fourth Test against the West Indies on day four, a Sunday. It was a long time since we had won a series against this formidable side and we were already 2-1 down this time around. In this match England had achieved a significant first innings lead, but the West Indies had fought back on day three, reaching 159 for the loss of three wickets with their two top batsmen, Richie Richardson and Brian Lara, building a strong partnership. However, almost as soon as we settled into our seats something amazing started to happen.

In the very first over of the day Dominic Cork clean bowled the West Indian captain Richardson and followed up next ball by dismissing Junior Murray. Cork was now steaming into Carl Hooper in search of his hat-trick. At precisely the wrong moment a 'Barmy Army' cheerleader sat just in front of us rose to his feet with his back to the cricket to exalt his troops to raise the decibel levels a further notch in support of Cork.

It seemed to do the trick as Carl Hooper was trapped leg before wicket to give Cork the first hat-trick by an Englishman for many years. Unfortunately, Roy and I could only deduce what had happened from the wild celebrations of everyone around us. Our view had been completely obscured by the unofficial Barmy Army general. It was hard to bear.

Roy had already developed a degree of antipathy towards the chap in question as, instead of wearing traditional cricket watching clobber, he was adorned in a Manchester United shirt with 'Cantona Kung Fu Fighter' emblazoned on the back. This was presumably in support of Eric Cantona, who had earlier in the year delivered a kung-fu kick into the chest of Crystal Palace fan Matthew Simmons during a stormy match at Selhurst Park.

Roy's first reaction was to threaten to throw the guy off the balcony. I felt obliged to point out that this would result in the man's certain death and a charge of murder, although Roy remained adamant that he would be pardoned on compassionate grounds.

'Most magistrates and judges love cricket,' he maintained.

Starting to calm down, he addressed the culprit in a more measured tone.

'You realise that was the first hat-trick by an England player since 1957 and thanks to you I didn't see it!'

'Christ, mate, you must be old to remember that. Who was it, WG Grace?'

Roy looked at him with disdain. 'Peter Loader against the West Indies at Leeds. He took the last three wickets and England won by an innings.'

Yet again I was amazed at Roy's knowledge of past cricketers.

'Never 'eard of 'im!' the lad replied.

'Hardly surprising. You're a football supporter.' As far as Roy was concerned that said it all. 'No self-respecting sports fan would celebrate a professional player kicking a fan in the chest,' he added, slightly pompous now.

'He wasn't a very nice bloke, the Palace fan,' the guy pointed out in defence of his United hero.

'So I understand,' Roy conceded. 'I wouldn't have minded so much if he had punched him, not given him a bloody kicking!'

I felt that Roy was beginning to lose the thread of his argument, even conceding the moral high ground, but I said nothing.

'He did punch him as well, a tidy right-handed jab it was,' the lad said proudly.

'Well why didn't you put that on your stupid shirt?'

The lad looked bemused. 'I'll tell you what, let me buy you a pint,' he suggested.

'Mine's a bitter,' said Roy with reasonable grace. 'And so is my brother's.'

The lad looked at me pleadingly. Two pints at stadium prices was a big outlay.

I wasn't very helpful. 'Real ale mind, none of that fizzy shite.'

As is Roy's way, an hour and a few pints later they were friends, laughing together at the stream of male and female streakers who ran on to the pitch in defiance of the fact it was Our Lord's day. As England clinched a memorable victory later that evening the two pals were hugging each other.

How could you hold a grudge against a passionate cricket fan? Roy had crossed the line and become a Barmy Army supporter, at least in spirit. I, on the other hand, remained sceptical, although it was always only a matter of time.

Following this incident we had little direct contact with members of the Barmy Army. They were an increasing presence at every international match that we attended, usually in a different stand to us, and our view of them could best be described as 'benign'. We found most of their songs funny and their support, often in the face of adversity, commendable. We certainly found Christopher Martin-Jenkins' remark that they were 'demeaning English cricket' terribly over the top. Any organisation whose *raison d'etre* was to 'make watching cricket more fun and much more popular' was okay with us.

Over time they really did start to alter the way cricket supporters behaved and through them watching cricket has become more fun. For example, a huge number of fans now turn up at matches in fancy dress, often with large groups dressed according to an agreed theme. The sight of ten Friar Tucks sitting in a row or 25 Santa doing a conga brings a smile to the lips of even the most traditional cricket supporters. Particularly on the Saturday of a Test match, now widely regarded as 'fancy dress day', the television cameras spend a lot of time picking out the best and most ridiculous costumes. And, as the Barmy Army hoped, watching England play live cricket both at home and abroad is now more popular than it has ever been, even though in other ways cricket is failing to reach a wider audience.

I remember the Barmy Army being very vocal in the 2005 Ashes, although in the final stages of the fourth Test at Trent Bridge I think they were as quiet as the rest of us. It was hard to sing and shout, other than in pain, as Shane Warne, ably assisted by Brett Lee, threatened everyone's sanity.

However, when we toured Australia in 2006 the Barmy Army suddenly became very significant to us. We had booked our trip with a different touring company and they did a perfectly efficient job. Each day of the match in Brisbane we found ourselves in the same two seats amongst the same group of England fans who were knowledgeable about the game, pleasant and polite and perfectly good company. But it soon became evident that the tone amongst England fans was being set by those who had travelled with the Barmy Army.

Right from the start, from the first ball in fact, things went wrong for our team. For the Barmy Army this was not a problem; in fact it cast them in the role that they had so willingly adopted at their inaugural Ashes Test series back in 1994/95, that of gallant losers smiling in the face of adversity.

The Barmy Army songbook was by then quite extensive with a song dedicated to many players, past and present and at Brisbane they were in full voice, although the songs that sprang up spontaneously were often the best. They are not great respecters of reputation and there were a few occasions when they adopted a chant about a player that was based on the flimsiest of facts. I have no intention of perjuring myself by giving examples.

The Australian fans, whilst admiring the irony and wit of the Barmy Army, often objected to the songs about their heroes. However, this only spurred the Barmy Army on to make further even more outrageous claims about the most popular Australian players. The desire of the Australian fans to 'set the record straight' even followed us up the Sunshine Coast where we stayed for a few days before returning home. We would be sitting on the beach or having a beer when a group of earnest Australians would approach us to insist the text of the various songs and chants were totally incorrect. We always reacted as loyal Barmy Army foot soldiers, insisting that the chants were based on well-established facts!

Any Australian who dropped a catch or mis-fielded the ball was immediately rewarded with about five hours of concentrated attention from the Army, an honour indeed.

As England went down with only fleeting moments of resistance the Barmy Army said in song what every Australian in the ground now knew to be true:

'We are the army, the Barmy Army
Oh we are bonkers, and we are mad.
We are the loyalist cricket supporters
That the world has ever had.'

Despite the fact that one of the Army's cruellest songs 'Yesterday' is about the Australian ex-captain Ricky Ponting, he is himself a fan. On one occasion, at the Oval in 2005, he responded with some humour of his own.

England, who just needed a draw to win the Ashes, were benefiting from bad light that caused the umpires to bring the teams on and off the pitch using up precious time.

The Barmy Army in a humorous attempt to influence the umpires all held umbrellas aloft although it wasn't raining. Soon after play was interrupted for bad light. Later the umpires decided the light had improved slightly and, to yet another rendition of 'Jerusalem', Ponting led Australia back on to the field with the whole team wearing sunglasses despite the less than bright conditions. The Barmy Army roared their appreciation.

The Australian fans have tried to respond through a supporters' group known as the 'Fanatics'.

Although they often lack the self-deprecating ironic humour of the Barmy Army, they have had their moments. In response to the Barmy Army song, 'You all live in a convict colony', sung to the tune of 'Yellow Submarine', the Fanatics now sometimes come dressed appropriately.

Not surprisingly, the England players absolutely love the Barmy Army and they invariably acknowledge them at the end of a Test match, win or lose. In his book, *On Fire* published in 2019, Ben Stokes makes it clear how important the Army is to him and his fellow players.

Describing scenes at the end of the victorious World Cup Final he wrote: 'Halfway round our Lord's lap, we got to where the Barmy Army were gathered in the Compton Stand of the Nursery End. This was a big part of our celebrations … Why, because these folk are quite simply the best supporters in the world. In any sport. They follow us all over, through thick and thin, never giving up on us.'[4]

To Ben Stokes that is the definition of a true fan. Their support is unconditional, something that opposition fans are unable to fully grasp.

In January 2020 the Barmy Army celebrated their 25th anniversary and the reaction from the cricket media was also universally positive. Michael Vaughan, ex-England captain and cricket pundit, summed up the general view in cricket that the Army is great for the game.

'Cricket is fighting with many other sports for exposure. And they provide atmosphere and provide the team so much support. The humour and the way they behave is fantastic. If anyone is out of hand they deal with it themselves. They're self-policed. It's testimony to what they're about.'

Like Stokes he then went on to emphasise the unconditional support they offer their team.

'And they support through good and bad. They've seen the best and the worst and they're always the same, they're singing and dancing and trying to create an atmosphere. And when the Barmy Army's singing, the team so often gets a wicket. They really are the England team's 12th man.'

Chapter 18

Barmy in South Africa

THIRTEEN YEARS after our sojourn to Australia we felt we had at least one more tour in us. We settled on the idea of visiting Cape Town for the New Year Test against South Africa in 2020. After being somewhat detached from the mainstream in Australia in 2006 we had decided to go to the other extreme and travel as part of the Barmy Army. Fearing the worst but hoping for the best, it was with some trepidation that we boarded the Barmy Army chartered flight at Heathrow. If you are flying for 12 hours then boarding the plane in the late evening and arriving the following morning has some obvious advantages. However, when I suggested to friends that I would be able to sleep on a Barmy Army chartered flight my hopes were met with derision.

Once we were in the air and the seat belt signs had been switched off the crew started to move between us offering drinks. The norm seemed to be to order double gin and tonics, a beer and two small bottles of wine to go with the meal. It was now about 9.30 in the evening. Although not fans of binge drinking, Roy and I followed suit. Most people downed all of this before the food arrived and by 10.30pm the majority of the passengers were semi-comatose. By 11.30pm most were asleep. This suited me just fine and fears that Billy Cooper, the trumpet player for the Barmy Army, would be leading us in song for the whole flight soon receded.

We were put up in a number of large hotels in the centre of town that had been almost completely taken over by the Barmy Army. There were three or four days to fill before the cricket started and the Army offered daily tours to see the highlights of Cape Town and the surrounding area. Roy and I had made the decision beforehand to look around ourselves and we got to know the city in our own way. We took canal tours, open top bus trips, visited the V & A Waterfront and had lunch sitting in the sun at a variety of venues. Cape Town is a beautiful city with the aptly named Table Mountain dominating the landscape. The beaches and waterfronts are magnificent. However, despite the beauty of the region we had come to watch cricket and were more than ready when the first day finally arrived.

There is something special about supporting your team abroad, a feeling that I am sure is shared by football and rugby fans. However, watching a five-day Test with all its ups and downs, twists and turns is a unique experience and what a Test match we were treated to! Planning for the trip Roy and I had often said to each other that we would enjoy ourselves whatever the outcome, but oh the joy of victory! We were there to witness the first England win in Cape Town since 1957 and did so as part of the best and most knowledgeable set of supporters anywhere in the world. As two cricket purists we were grateful to witness the maiden century of a young man, Dominic Sibley, who at last understood the role of an opening batsman. Indeed, he not only understood it, but seemed to revel in it, embodying our memories of orthodox openers of the past.

At the end we cheered as loud as any as Stokes claimed the last three wickets amid the passionate chants of the Barmy Army, apparently believing they could carry their team to victory by sheer force of will.

It doesn't matter whether you follow cricket, cycling or curling the pleasure of such moments is only understood by sports fans. We felt truly blessed and I was glad to capture the joy on Roy's face as his team came good 6,000 miles from home.

* * *

In terms of their organisation our tour operators were anything but 'barmy' and everything ran smoothly until our arrival at the ground on the fourth day. A railway line ran alongside the ground and once we had got off the bus each day we had to reach the ground on foot via an underpass below the railway line. On day four we reached the underpass to find it flooded and impassable. Ground stewards were on hand to show us an alternative route, but we were rather surprised when they sent us across the railway lines.

Some of our contingent at first refused to cross, no doubt spooked by the fact that all the lights that guide the trains into the station were on green!

It was a long operation and one of the stewards stopped and sat down on the lines in a rather bizarre attempt to demonstrate the safety of the endeavour. Eventually everyone got across.

* * *

Being very interested in politics, Roy and I were interested to see what progress the country had made since the end of apartheid. It is sad to say that the economic factors that adversely affect black South Africans show no sign of real improvement. In 2020 at least one quarter of South

Africans live on less than 1.25 US dollars per day. The rate of unemployment remains doggedly above 25 per cent and is even rising slightly. The unemployment rate for young people is considerably higher. The nine years under the rule of President Zuma have been largely wasted with high levels of corruption and no significant economic progress. The beggars and homeless people on the streets of Cape Town bear testament to the many problems faced by black South Africans. So what is the legacy of the post-apartheid period? In terms of poverty, unemployment and equality all targets have been missed, but this is not to say nothing has changed.

You cannot get real insight into a city, let alone a country, in a short visit as a tourist, but there were many positive features about Cape Town which are likely attributable to unification. Everywhere you go in Cape Town you find a pride in the city and in the country that seems to say this is my South Africa. The people are so friendly and full of the joy of life. They hold conversations with friends on the other side of the street, shouting and smiling. Black South Africans laugh a lot and love to dance. There is a real respect between people of different races and they deal with each other with genuine politeness. I never once witnessed any bullish behaviour from Afrikaners towards blacks which I must say I had anticipated. I saw young couples from different racial backgrounds arm in arm and mixed groups of young people out together for the evening. Subsequent political regimes have done little to honour Nelson Mandela's ambitions regarding the eradication of poverty and reductions in inequality, but in terms of love, respect and human dignity his legacy appears to live on.

Returning to the UK in the middle of winter with Storm Brendan in full force, bringing rain and 80mph winds to parts of the country, was a shock to the system to say the least. However, it is amazing how quickly you return to your former way of life. Nevertheless, our experience in Cape Town was something that we will both treasure for a long time.

Chapter 19

The Laws of an Eccentric Game and the Spirit of Cricket

AS A left-handed pace bowler, I was always irritated by the lbw rule that states if the ball pitches outside the leg stump then it is not out. This applies even if the ball hits the batsman in line and would have gone on to hit the stumps. A left-handed bowler delivers the ball from outside the line of leg stump. If he/she is aiming at the stumps then it is almost inevitable that a high percentage of deliveries will pitch marginally outside leg. On the other hand, a right-handed bowler will likely pitch the ball outside off but can still be given an lbw decision. This is patently unfair.

I remember pointing this out to our cricket coach at my secondary school and asking for an explanation.

'It's the rules!' was his rather terse reply. Then after a moment's reflection he added, 'It works both ways. As a left-hander you're unlikely to get an lbw decision against you when you're batting.'

'But I bat No.11 and I'm a right-handed batsman anyway,' I replied indignantly.

He looked me up and down rather in the way that Captain Mainwaring looks at Private Pike in *Dad's Army*.

'Well, if you're left-handed and bat as a right-hander then you're more stupid than I thought!'

This was not entirely fair. Having been encouraged by my dad to bat left-handed, as he did, I was somewhat surprised at the reaction of my junior school PE teacher.

'Hold the thing properly, lad. You'll never connect with the ball otherwise.'

'I'm left-handed, sir.'

'Just because you can't hold a pen in the correct hand, doesn't mean you have to bat like a penguin.'

With that he walked across to me and readjusted my stance with a slap on the head as a reminder not to err again. I didn't.

In July 2018 Roy and I were sitting at Trent Bridge watching Nottinghamshire play Surrey. We had been looking forward to the game as Notts had made an excellent start to the season and Surrey were one of the fancied teams. Surrey had used the new rule that gave the away team the option of asking their opponents to bat first, thus doing away with the need for the toss.

Surrey had strengthened their already tidy seam attack by the addition of South African legend Morne Morkel. He proved just too good for the Notts batsmen, taking four wickets as the home team slumped to 210 all out in just 54 overs. This brought the Surrey captain and opener, Rory Burns, to the wicket. Burns was an extremely unorthodox left-hander who had been busy accumulating a lot of runs and attracting attention from the England set-up in their perpetual search for an effective opener.

Despite a very idiosyncratic batting style, Burns soon started scoring at a brisk rate.

'It must be hard to know how to bowl to him,' Roy observed. 'He moves that much in his crease you don't know what his plan is until it's too late.'

'Looks like a candidate for leg before,' I replied.

'Not with two right-arm opening bowlers. It's almost impossible to get an lbw decision against a leftie.'

Instantly this reactivated my grievance about the lbw law.

'Poor things! You want to try getting a decision as a left-arm bowler faced with a whole team of right-handed batsmen. It's bloody impossible.'

Roy looked a bit surprised at my level of feeling.

'That cricket writer Jonathan Liew is on your side. I read an article[6] he wrote a while ago now arguing for getting rid of the rule by which you can't be out leg before if it pitches outside leg.'

'Bloody right too. It's not going to help me though. I don't think I'm about to make a comeback at 60-odd!'

'He put up a good argument,' Roy maintained, 'but funnily enough he didn't mention you.'

There was a pause as I attempted a recovery from my brother's acerbic wit.

'So what did he say?'

'It was quite straightforward really,' Roy began. 'The bowler's job is to try and hit the wicket. The batsman's job is to use his bat to score runs and, if the bowler is accurate, to use it to stop the ball hitting the wicket. The lbw law is there to stop batters blocking it with their legs. If blocking it prevents the ball from hitting the wicket they should be given out.'

'I couldn't agree more,' I replied.

'He did go through the history of the lbw law, but in essence that was his argument.'

Later that day, as Burns and his opening partner Mark Stoneman piled on the runs, Roy found the article on his phone. Roy had summed it up pretty well, but because Jonathan Liew's language is somewhat more creative than Roy's I have quoted a short section of his article:

'If the ball is going on to hit the stumps, why should it matter where it went on its journey? Why should it matter that it pitched outside leg stump, or hit the batsman outside the line? It's because cricket was largely codified in Victorian Britain, and so here and there it retains certain remnants of that age: in this case, the Empire-era orthodoxy that the off side is pure and holy, the side of gentlemen, and the leg side is vulgar, uncouth and very possibly Bolshevik.'[6]

I agree with him to some extent, but I prefer Jimmy Anderson's simpler statement that I quote in an earlier chapter:

'Every single conceivable law in cricket is devised so that it suits the batsman.'[3]

I found to my cost another example of this self-evident truth when playing for the school team aged about 14. Like most young lads who wanted to be bowlers I concentrated on bowling as fast as I could even though as a result I often sacrificed both line and length. My other main priority was to perfect my appeal. A simple 'Howzat' never seemed enough and I had been studiously developing a primeval guttural cry as a means of appealing for a wicket.

During this game I had appealed in this manner on three occasions in one over. I was seeking an lbw decision that, given what I explained earlier, was never likely to be upheld. On the third rendition of my exaggerated 'Howzat' the umpire put his hands to his ears.

'If you carry on yelling at me in that way you're never going to get a decision. Just button it.'

On the final delivery of the over the batsman attempted a sweep shot but got a top edge and the ball was caught at midwicket. The umpire stood resolute, giving no signal to indicate the batsman was out. The batsman was not sure what was going on and, too timid to ask, just stayed in his crease. I was dumbfounded.

Before the other bowler went to start the next over I politely asked Mr Grumpy why he had not given the boy out.

'You didn't appeal,' he said.

'But you told me to button it,' I complained.

The umpire was enjoying himself. 'I told you to stop screaming in my ear. The batsman stayed in his ground so, regardless of how obvious it is that a wicket has been taken, you need to appeal. If you don't ask the question I can't raise my finger to declare him out.'

I suppose he thought he was teaching me a lesson and I guess he did. According to the laws of cricket he was right, but surely it was a bit harsh. I was only a kid.

There are 42 'Laws' (always written with a capital L) governing cricket and most of these Laws are sub-divided into many individual rules. As a result there are literally hundreds of rules covering the game. Many of these will be familiar to anyone with a passing interest in cricket, but there are some which are quite obscure and rarely applied.

My wife is German and has no affinity whatsoever to cricket, but even she knows that if the bowler sends down a delivery and it either hits the stumps or is hit in the air and caught by a fielder, the batsman is out. Incidentally, 'out bowled' is covered reasonably simply by Law 32. 'Out caught' is covered by Law 33 but requires 11 sub-rules to clarify the situation.

There are, however, many other forms of dismissal that rarely arise and can send umpires in recreational cricket into a spin.

Take Law 34: 'The striker is out hit the ball twice if, while the ball is in play, it strikes any part of his/her person or is struck by his/her bat and, before the ball has been touched by a fielder, the striker wilfully strikes it again except for the purpose of guarding his/her wicket.'

You will sometimes see young kids new to the sport defend the ball with their bat and, as it sits temptingly on the pitch in front of them, give it a firm belt and set off for a run. I remember my grandson Finlay doing this when I first introduced him to the game aged about four. This Law exists primarily to outlaw this practice. However, it gets more complicated. The batsman is *not* out if they hit the ball a second time in order to return it to a fielder, but beware! In Law 37 it states:

'A batsman is out obstructing the field if, at any time while the ball is in play and, *without the consent of a fielder*, he/she uses the bat or any part of his/her person to return the ball to any fielder.'

Another obscure form of dismissal is 'out handling the ball'. A batsman can be given out for handling the ball if, while playing a delivery, the batsman intentionally touches the ball with one or both of their hands not holding the bat, unless done to avoid incurring an injury. Up until 2017 there was a separate Law covering this, but it is now subsumed into the Law relating to obstructing the field. However, handling the ball still gets you out.

In 1993 Graham Gooch became the only player to be dismissed for handling the ball after scoring a century. Playing defensively to try and draw the Test match against Australia, Gooch blocked a short ball from Merv Hughes. The ball flicked off his bat and fell towards his stumps, prompting Gooch to instinctively punch the ball away. He was given out and Australia went on to win the match.

Since the adoption of helmets a new Law has been introduced. You will often see wicketkeepers wearing a helmet when the pace bowlers are on, but remove it if a fast bowler is replaced by a spinner. Fine, he puts it on the ground behind him, dons his cap and the game goes on. So what happens if the batsman hits the ball and it strikes the helmet lying there on the ground? In a Law that surely vindicates Jimmy Anderson's view that 'every single conceivable law in cricket is devised so that it suits the batsman'[3], the batsman is awarded five runs!

Possibly the most important part of the Laws is the preamble that deals with the spirit of cricket.

'Cricket owes much of its appeal and enjoyment to the fact that it should be played not only according to the Laws, but also within the Spirit of Cricket ... Respect is central to the Spirit of Cricket. Respect your captain, team-mates, opponents and the authority of the umpires.'

One of the most iconic moments in the intense rivalry of the Ashes demonstrates this spirit in practice. At the end of the thrilling second Ashes Test at Edgbaston in 2005 Australian Brett Lee had almost taken his team to a most unlikely victory but fell just three runs short. He fell to his knees in despair and was comforted by England's Andrew Flintoff, who put a consoling arm around him and helped him to his feet.

In an interview about the incident Flintoff says, 'Growing up as a cricketer for Lancashire I was always taught that in victory or defeat you respect the opposition first.' He certainly demonstrated that respect in that moment of otherwise unbridled joy for him and his team-mates.

The spirit of the game is often invoked when a player is run out whilst backing up. As a bowler enters his delivery stride, the non-striking batsman usually 'backs up', i.e., he leaves his crease and walks towards the other end of the wicket so that it will take him less time to reach the other end in the event of a run being called. If just at the point that he would have delivered the ball the bowler notices the batsman at his end is already out of his crease he is entitled to run him out.

This is often referred to as the Mankad rule, named after Indian bowler Vinoo Mankad, who created controversy when he dismissed Australian batsman Bill Brown twice in a similar manner at the Sydney Cricket Ground in a 1947 Test.

I was always aware of this rule as a young bowler but had been firmly taught that to remove a batsman in this way was not in the spirit of the game. On those occasions where the batsman was over-zealous in his backing up I did sometimes hold the ball over the bails and politely suggest he was taking the mick. If a bowler warned the batsman in this way and he persisted I doubt whether any criticism would fall on the bowler if he subsequently applied the Mankad rule. However, I don't recall ever doing this.

In 2019 in the Indian Premier League Ravi Ashwin ran out Rajasthan Royals player Jos Buttler at the non-striker's end in this fashion as the Englishman wandered out of his crease just prior to Ashwin's delivery. Buttler was forced to depart the scene and he exchanged angry words with Ashwin as he left the field amid a chorus of boos from the crowd. Later, several prominent ex-players pitched into the debate led by Shane Warne.

'As captain of your side you set the standard of the way the team wants to play and what the team stands for! Why do such a disgraceful and low act like that tonight? You must live with yourself and it's too late to say sorry. You will be remembered for that low act.'

Royals' coach Paddy Upton, who exchanged words with Ashwin at the conclusion of the match, should probably have the last word.

'I think we'll leave it up to the IPL fans to decide if that's the kind of thing they want to see and we'll leave it up to the cricket world to judge Ashwin's actions tonight.'

I know where I stand.

Finally, the spirit of the game is very much in play on those occasions when a batsman is declared out, but the captain of the fielding team withdraws the appeal. To do this the captain needs the consent of the umpire, although it is unlikely to be withheld. For example, if a batsman collides with a fielder and is left stranded in the middle while the opposing team removes the bails to run him out such a mode of dismissal may not be deemed as within the spirit of cricket and the captain may recall him.

Roy and I were at Trent Bridge in 2011 watching a Test between England and India when the most famous example of this took place. Ian Bell had already reached a century when with the last ball before tea he appeared to have hit a boundary. With this satisfying end to the session Bell turned and headed for the pavilion for tea. As it turned out the ball had not crossed the boundary rope and was still live. The ball was returned to the wicketkeeper and with Bell halfway to the pavilion he was run out.

We and the whole crowd vented our spleen throughout the interval, talking darkly about how the game had let itself down. As the Indian team took the field again after tea they were roundly booed by the crowd including us. However, the boos soon turned to applause as Ian Bell emerged from the pavilion to continue his fine innings, India's captain MS Dhoni having withdrawn the appeal. Nine years later in December 2020 Dhoni's tremendous gesture was recognised when he was announced as the unanimous winner of the ICC Spirit of Cricket Award of the Decade.

Chapter 20

Are All Wicketkeepers Nuts?

ABOUT TWO years ago, when my grandson Finlay was first showing promise as a cricketer, the coach asked him if he wanted to have a try out behind the stumps. Even aged ten it was obvious that Fin was a good fielder and equally clear that he wanted to be involved in the game at every turn. As I was driving him and Iris home after training he asked me what I thought of the idea. I must admit that I was inclined to encourage him.

Wicketkeepers are central to every team, involved throughout and often relied on by their colleagues, particularly their captain and bowlers. If they are half decent they will always get a game. There is no cricket team without a wicketkeeper.

Finlay himself was keen too. I think he liked the idea of throwing himself about in a theatrical manner to the applause of his team-mates and onlookers. I had noticed that when we practised catching he would dive for balls he could better catch standing up. In fact, I had been trying to discourage this in him, stressing that most catches are taken when the fielder has managed to set him/herself in a stable and balanced position.

About two days after he had been asked about wicketkeeping we were playing catch on the lawn when I reminded him not to keep diving. Marieluise who knows nothing about cricket was passing as I said it.

'Leave him alone, he's just having fun,' she said.

At first I dismissed her remarks, but in truth it made an impact on me. Of course, there is one big downside to being the wicketkeeper: once you take the job, you're stuck with it and your chances of 'having fun' are sacrificed to concentration and work ethic. At ten years of age you should be enjoying every aspect of the game. Wisely, after talking to his dad, Fin decided against it. It was not long before I realised that securing a place in the team was never likely to be a problem for Finlay. He is a very good batsman and a reliable bowler besides being an outstanding fielder.

All this set me thinking about how people become wicketkeepers and the next time we went to watch Nottinghamshire, I raised it with Roy.

'Well, the essential starting point is you have to be nuts!' he told me, as if this were self-evident.

'Finlay is anything but nuts, Iris maybe, but not Fin,' I replied.

'Well, there you have it. He'll never make it as a wicketkeeper. And don't let him be tempted into being a keeper in football either. Goalies are all bonkers too.'

'Has this theory been tested?' I enquired.

'Tested? Think of all the great wicketkeepers during our lifetime. If not actually nuts they were certainly eccentric.'

I started to list them in my mind, but Roy was off on one now.

'Think of Jack Russell, one of the best, possibly the best ever. Did you know that when he had an extension built on his house he insisted all the builders were blindfolded en route so they couldn't find out where he lived?'

'You're making this up!' I protested. 'Maybe he's just a very private person.'

'He's at the very least eccentric!'

We recalled when we first started watching Nottinghamshire in the County Championship. Whatever the state of the game the wicketkeeper, Chris Read, would run to the other end of the pitch at the conclusion of each over and then look around to see whether all the other fielders were ready. Inevitably, they weren't.

As we continued our conversation other spectators sitting around us started to chip in with their nutty wicketkeeper anecdotes. One sitting just in front of us wanted to draw the conversation back to Jack Russell.

'Did you know that when in the middle of one of his extreme fitness regimes, he had a diet consisting largely of tea, biscuits and baked beans?'

I hadn't heard this, but inevitably Roy knew all about Russell's bizarre diet.

'He loved his tea. He'd often get through 20 cups a day using just one tea bag. He used to dip the tea bag in once, add milk, then hang it on a nail ready to use it for the next cup. In the final Test of the '89 Ashes Derek Randall reckons he used the same bag for all five days. Mind you, Randall was pretty quirky himself.'

Our new-found friend looked sceptical but was not to be outdone.

'In the old days players used to look forward to the lunches, didn't they? Some grounds were renowned for what they served up, but Jack Russell wasn't interested. Apparently he would eat two Weetabix, soaked for exactly eight minutes in milk, and a mashed banana.'

Roy turned to me as if his point had been proven.

'See what I mean, completely eccentric.'

The man in front of us was not finished yet.

'I'm sure you know he was obsessed with staying fit and free of injuries.'

Roy nodded sagely while I feigned interest. The man continued.

'Driving between games he would be clad in a sleeping bag with the bottom cut out, so as not to get a chill in his back and legs. He also had a block fitted beneath the accelerator, so as to avoid over-stretching the Achilles tendon.'

I felt the need to add something to the conversation before we got on to whether he slept on his back or his side.

'The only daft thing I know about him is he always wore that battered old flowerpot hat, for the whole of his career they reckon.'

This was my only contribution, but Roy and his new chum looked decidedly unimpressed. I guess every cricket fan knew about the hat, but I doubt whether they knew about the brushes he had with the cricket authorities on account of it. I was soon to be informed.

'When he was playing for England he was always getting into trouble over the state of the bloody thing,' said Roy.

'Yeh, that's true. He must've thought it was like a lucky charm,' our pal replied. 'When England were touring South Africa Russell refused to wear the official coloured one-day sun hat. Eventually he agreed to wear it as long as he could wear his old flowerpot under it.'

Roy shook his head slowly. 'Very odd!'

However, the final word on Jack Russell went to our new friend.

'He must've rated himself as a keeper,' he began.

'How do you make that out?' Roy enquired, slightly aggrieved that one of his heroes was suddenly being painted as arrogant.

'He's asked if his hands can be amputated after his death and preserved in formaldehyde.'

Well, what more could you say?

* * *

I have only ever played behind the stumps once and it is not a job that I would put my hand up for again. I was captaining our trade union team when for two overs in a row our wicketkeeper, who bizarrely always turned out in red football shorts, dropped almost every ball. At the end of the second over I went and asked him if there was a problem.

'It's this sodding gout,' he informed me. 'It's bloody killing me!'

I carefully examined his eyes and nose for signs of excessive port consumption, but other than a slightly runny nose, noticed nothing untoward.

'I can't carry on,' he announced pulling off his gloves and unbuckling his pads. 'You'll have to do it.' And with that he left the field.

Reluctantly I took up my new position. I only did it for 18 overs but by the end of the innings my hands were red raw and stinging like mad. It was therefore surprising to learn that one of England's finest wicketkeepers, Bob Taylor, wore Mitre wicketkeeping gloves from which he cut away all the padding from inside the palms and removed the webbing. His reasoning for this was that he liked to feel the ball in his palm. He maintained that if you took the ball correctly the bruising would not be too troublesome. Obviously I had been doing something wrong!

* * *

Often when watching a county game Roy and I go up to the restaurant at the top of the Radcliffe Road Stand for lunch. On this occasion I was not keen on the idea as the chap in the seat in front of us would almost certainly have joined us. He was a nice enough guy, but I already knew more about Jack Russell than his own mother and I was not sure I could take any more. I suggested to Roy that we go for a walk and pick up a sandwich at the Co-op to which he reluctantly agreed.

When we returned for the afternoon session I put it to Roy we might sit on the opposite side of the ground to get a different perspective. I'm sure he knew what was behind this suggestion. Consequently, he just grinned and nodded his approval.

The game was slow, Roy was sipping his tea which seemed to have a somewhat soporific effect on him, and I found myself considering what he had said about goalies. I could think of a few English keepers who were pretty eccentric, but none came close to the Colombian goalkeeper René Higuita.

Higuita was famous for running out of his goal with the ball at his feet, sometimes beating opposition players as he went. On many occasions he suddenly realised he was 50 yards or more from his goal and went haring back. However, none of this compared to his antics against England at Wembley in 1995. With the ball coming towards his goal, instead of catching it he executed a 'scorpion kick' achieved by diving forwards, placing his hands on the ground and lunging his heels forward above his head to kick the ball.

The following morning Terry Wogan reported with obvious glee that an amateur coach had manfully tried to demonstrate the kick to his under-11s team and had been taken to hospital with a broken shoulder.

You can make a similar analogy between wicketkeepers and drummers. The lonely drummer, the isolated musician at the back, and yet the engine room and driving force of any band. Often the most interesting character, eccentric, loners, often plain barmy and yet the band couldn't exist without them. They are characters, but like wicketkeepers although indispensable they remain in the background behind the flamboyant characters in 'the front line-up'. The singers, like the batsmen, are the headline grabbers, the recognisable names, often egocentric, imbued with notoriety.

* * *

One thing I admire about Roy is his ability to keep hold of his mug of tea even when he nods off. When he does suddenly wake up he usually starts speaking immediately to cover the fact he has been dozing. However, on this occasion the small puddle on the ground just below his mug gave the game away.

'I've been thinking about other keepers,' he began, unaware that my thought processes had passed beyond wicketkeepers, through goalies to drummers. As my memory finally delivered the name of Cream's eccentric drummer: (Ginger Baker), I tried to get my mind back to the subject of our discussion.

'I don't know much about him, but that guy Paul Nixon who played for Leicestershire, he was pretty strange as well,' Roy continued.

'Yes, I remember him. Right at the end of his career he played for England in a load of limited-over games over just a few months. He was fairly odd. He literally never stopped talking.'

Roy took a last suck of his tea, screwing his face up as he did so. It must have been stone cold.

'It was aimed at the batsman, but it wasn't really sledging, more just friendly banter. The trouble was it never stopped. Must've driven the batsmen mad.'

'I assume that was the idea,' I replied. 'I think he was trying to spoil their concentration. Probably worked.'

We both fell silent for a while as the game drifted on towards an inevitable draw. One of the pleasures of watching cricket is that you can do it in complete silence or you can hold an animated conversation, not necessarily about cricket, without losing track of what is happening on the pitch. If something significant happens in the game Roy will stop in mid-sentence until the excitement has passed. Then after a sharp intake of breath between clenched teeth creating an audible hiss he will continue with whatever point he was previously trying to make. On this occasion Luke Fletcher, one of the Notts pace bowlers, had appealed for lbw but the umpire had given the batsman 'not out'.

Roy made that familiar sound, like a car mechanic who is responding to your question, 'how much will it cost'.

'Looked out to me,' he exclaimed, although all sports fans will recognise this as a statement of partisanship rather than an objective observation.

'Bloody plumb if you ask me,' he added.

'I've been watching Chris Read,' he announced back on theme. 'I suppose concentrating intently on every ball for hours on end probably encourages a certain quirkiness.'

'Yeh, I suppose so. It's a thankless task, right enough,' I replied. 'So, who do you rate as the best ever?'

Roy's answer was immediate. 'Has to be Godfrey Evans.'

I should not have been surprised. It was inevitable that my brother would nominate a dead cricketer.

'How do you make that out?' I enquired rather pugnaciously. 'You were only ten when he retired!'

'I saw enough,' he stated as if the subject were now closed.

'Well, dad watched him through his whole career and he believed Alan Knott was better.'

I was not sure at the time and am still uncertain whether our dad actually said this, but it suited my purpose. Certainly, he was a great admirer of Knott.

'Now you're really talking about an eccentric wicketkeeper. Alan Knott was certainly the most quirky. I'll give you that.'

We had both seen Knott many times and he certainly gave that impression. Many colleagues and cricket writers would testify to his eccentricity. However, I remember an interview after he retired when he told a great story about Middlesex's West Indian pace bowler, Wayne Daniel. Daniel was a huge man and bowled at the speed of light. Apparently Daniel bowled him a bouncer, then asked him if he could play in his benefit match in September. 'Let me think about it,' replied Knott. Next ball was another vicious bouncer. 'I have thought about it. Put me down!' Knott shot back. This seemed eminently sensible.

A quality much admired in modern keepers is the ability to keep talking all day, rather in the style of Paul Nixon mentioned earlier. Knott, however, rarely had anything to say from behind the stumps. His eccentricities were of a different order.

As with Jack Russell he liked to wear a familiar hat, in his case a sun hat at first worn in sunny places like Australia, but later on at Derby and Old Trafford where it was an unnecessary precaution. As the years went on other idiosyncratic clothing became associated with Alan Knott, not least the handkerchief drooping from his left pocket.

Soon he stopped acquiring new pads and the old familiar ones became ever more baggy and were secured by tape. He always kept his shirt collar turned up to protect him from the sun and his sleeves rolled down to safeguard his elbows when diving. Touching the bails became an obsession, as did stretching between deliveries.

Knott's favourite drink at the end of the day's play was a pint of sherry and lemonade. He would drink the lemonade and leave the sherry that had inevitably sunk to the bottom of the glass.

He was, despite all the talk of his odd ways, regarded as one of the greatest wicketkeepers to ever play the game. He was described by cricket journalist Simon Wilde as 'a natural glove man, beautifully economical in his movements and armed with tremendous powers of concentration'.[8] Many team-mates and cricket journalists maintain that they never saw him drop a catch or miss a stumping chance. On top of everything else he was a superb batsman who rescued England from collapse on very many occasions. Was he the greatest ever? I believe my dad thought so and I am inclined to agree with him.

Chapter 21

England Batting Collapses, My Brother and Me

THROUGHOUT THIS book I have celebrated all the glorious moments that my brother and I have witnessed as England supporters. I have said that if you watch as many Test matches as we have then you are bound to be present on quite a few historic occasions when all England's stars align. And in this respect we have indeed been lucky.

I have recalled exhilarating innings by Ian Botham in the 1981 Ashes and by Kevin Pietersen against his country of birth at Leeds in 2012. I have tried to paint a picture of the hard-fought victory at Cape Town at the start of 2020 that turned the series. I have described the incredible hat-tricks by Dominic Cork and Stuart Broad and, best of them all, Stuart Broad's 8-15 in the Trent Bridge Ashes Test in 2015.

However, if you support the England cricket team for more than 50 years it is inevitable that you will witness some disasters too. At the risk of ending this book on a low point, it would be remiss of me not to refer to the agony and bewilderment that you feel when witnessing England's many spectacular batting collapses over the same period. So as not to depress the reader, or myself, too much I will confine my recollections to this century.

Roy and I had tickets for the first four days of England v Pakistan at Old Trafford in 2001. It is not easy finding campsites in reach of Old Trafford, and we ended up in a small town near the Peak District called Hazel Grove. It was about 15 miles from Old Trafford but had a rail link directly into the centre of Manchester.

It was only a two-match series and, although the two teams were thought to be fairly evenly matched, England had won the first Test by an innings and nine runs. We hoped to see England win this match as well and clinch the series.

It was a game dominated by the batsmen and we were lucky enough to witness excellent centuries by Michael Vaughan and Graham Thorpe for England and Inzamam-ul-Haq for Pakistan. About one and a half hours before close on the fourth day Pakistan were all out and England started their second innings requiring 370 to win. This was a challenging target, but a promising opening stand between Michael Atherton and Marcus Trescothick took England to 85 without loss at close, leaving a final day target of 285 with all ten wickets still in hand.

Roy and I had already taken Monday off work and so decided to stay on for the last day. The next morning Atherton and Trescothick continued their steady progress which was ended by a Waqar Younis yorker to Atherton. Although England were still well placed on 146/1 they instantly shut up shop with a view to getting a draw and sealing a series win. With the two centurions from the first innings, Vaughan and Thorpe, still to come as well as captain Alec Stewart and a strong tail, this seemed unnecessarily negative. Nevertheless, we took the change in attitude in our stride. Both England players and fans had got used to losing from this sort of position for most of the previous decade so ambitions were low.

It is obviously a very different game today and I could not imagine either the current England team giving up the chase so early or the fans putting up with it.

England continued their slow, ponderous progress and just after tea they had reached 201/2. Victory was now probably beyond them, but saving the game looked easy enough.

But it wasn't! England lost their last eight wickets for 60, on what was still a good wicket and Pakistan tied the series. The result was a fitting tribute to the skills of their formidable pace attack of Wasim Akram and Waqar and the tenacity of their spinner Saqlain Mushtaq, who got through 47 overs. They were greatly helped by Manchester's Pakistani population, who descended on Old Trafford during the afternoon, almost turning it into a home venue. Roy and I sat there traumatised; heads bowed.

In July 2017 my two grandchildren, Iris and Finlay, accompanied us to a Test match at Trent Bridge for the first time. They were only six and eight respectively but were already members of a local cricket club and so knew a bit about the game. Inevitably, Iris found the crowd and the venue more interesting than the cricket, but her parents had come well prepared with stickers, colouring books and other forms of quiet entertainment.

They had stuff to occupy Fin too, but it soon became clear that these distractions were not required. From the very first ball he was glued to the action and having quickly discovered that Roy had an encyclopaedic knowledge of cricket he asked endless questions, all of which were relevant to the state of the game. His dad Andy and I were used to this level of interrogation from Finlay and we were both happy to leave Roy to it.

We had tickets for days two, three and four and day two started with the completion of the South African innings reaching a respectable 335. From there the game went rapidly downhill with England scoring only 205 in a first innings lasting little more than 50 overs. The only consolation for Finlay was seeing his hero, Joe Root, hit 78 runs off just 76 balls. It was great fun while it lasted which sadly wasn't very long.

In their second innings South Africa batted well again and finally declared, leaving England an unlikely target of 474. We all did our best to get across to Fin that England were extremely unlikely to get there, but he was adamant they would.

Unfortunately, Finlay's optimism was misplaced and England collapsed to 133 all out in just 42 overs. The poor kid was devastated, and it took all our combined efforts to comfort him. I would have understood if he had never wanted to watch England again.

However, like a true fan he was back at the same venue almost exactly a year later with Roy, me, his family and my other daughter Lucy, ready to support his team. This time the opponents were India.

This was the third Test in a five-match series and England were already 2-0 up so hopes were high. On the first day we were separated from the others as Roy and I had opted to watch from the pavilion. Having won the toss England made the unusual decision to put India in. When the day closed with India on 307 for the loss of six wickets it was clear that the decision had not been vindicated. However, there were still plenty of opportunities for England to get back into the game.

During the course of the day Roy and I had chatted with the stewards about the possibility of Finlay and Iris coming into the pavilion before play with a view to trying to get some autographs. He and his sister each had one of those diddy bats and were hopeful that they might get close to a few players. As one would expect, the stewards were very helpful and told us to bring the children to the pavilion before ten the following morning.

At 9.45am on day two Roy and I arrived with Fin, Iris being too overawed to accompany us. Five minutes later we were seated alongside the steps leading from the pavilion on to the ground. Fin had his little bat at the ready while I had Iris's. It could not have gone better. The players were so friendly to Fin and soon both bats were covered in autographs.

In particular, Joe Root and Cheteshwar Pujara took time out to chat with him. Pujara, who had played for Nottinghamshire the previous season, even told Fin about the birth of his baby girl four months earlier.

Stuart Broad was in a hurry as he passed us but promised Fin he would find him when he returned to the pavilion. He was true to his word and made a point of looking out for Fin as he came back up the steps. My youngest daughter Lucy, who I am sure admires Stuart Broad for his cricketing ability alone, had told Fin to make sure he mentioned her when speaking to him. The meaning of this request was lost on Fin and he duly failed to complete his mission.

England started well with Broad and Anderson capturing the last four wickets for only six runs and Alastair Cook and Keaton Jennings taking England to lunch on 46/0 from just nine overs. And that was the end of the good news. By tea England were all out for 161 as Hardik Pandya took five wickets in the space of 29 deliveries. The game was effectively over. Fin had been unlucky again!

I have covered the Headingley Ashes Test in August 2019 in some detail in chapter seven. This is of course the Test match that ended with a world-beating innings by Ben

Stokes that miraculously took England to victory. However, England's abject surrender as they were bowled out for 67 in their first innings was without doubt mine and Roy's worst experience in 50 years of watching international cricket. The subsequent heroics from Ben Stokes, ably supported by Jack Leach, took place after we had returned home and unfortunately have not managed to wipe the memory of that worst of all collapses from our minds.

England have only been bowled out in a single session of a home Test match three times since 1938. Roy and I have seen two of them!

Chapter 22

The Nightwatchman

Nightwatchman – An Elegy –
Peter Carpenter [9]

Mouth set. So far, nought
not out, having dabbed at
the spinner who'd been giving it
some air. Hands soft – taking the sting
out of each delivery.

Their demon quickie
is brought back into the attack.
He pounds in.
A virtuoso leave.
You judge the away
swinger to perfection.

Shadows nudge further east
across the square. Pigeons clatter
as mid-off jogs back. Thunderous
approach to the wicket. This one
you nick.

The keeper whoops and hurls
the ball to the skies. You walk without waiting
for the dreaded finger.
Head-down trudge
to a sealed cube with the door marked
VISITORS. Dust motes patrol heated air.

In among the grim socks, grass-stained
whites and open coffins you take in
the smell of embrocation, shake off
gloves, stoop to unbuckle your pads.

Nightwatchman *by Peter Carpenter, from* After the
Goldrush *2009. Published by permission of Nine Arches Press.*
www.ninearchespress.com

On a bank holiday weekend, when Roy was about 16 and
virtually a regular in our dad's firm's team, he was asked by
the captain, Ken Sykes, to bat up the order. Roy normally
batted at eight or nine, but Ken wanted him to go in when
the next wicket fell. His team had won the toss and were
batting first. They had so far amassed nearly 80 runs for
the loss of just one wicket. Ken Sykes himself was next man
in. Roy sought some kind of explanation from his captain,
whom he held in high regard.

'What, am I some sort of nightwatchman?'

Ken looked at his watch. It was only 2.30pm and it was a
40-over game set to finish later that day. He concluded that
Roy had been watching too much cricket on telly.

'Don't be daft, lad. Just get your pads on. You're in next.'

Roy, a good team player, wanted to comply, but there
was a problem. The team only had three pairs of pads. The
two batsmen in the middle had two sets and Ken Sykes was

CRICKET, MY BROTHER AND ME

wearing the third pair. When Roy pointed this out he was unhelpful.

'Whoever's out next take his pads. You'll have them on in no time.'

At this Ken disappeared into the pavilion where our mum and Ivy Lunnon were busy preparing the tea, usually taken at the change of innings. Therein lay the reason for Ken's unexpected request.

'Given it's a bank holiday and most of the boys would probably prefer to be with their families, Ivy and I have made a special effort with the tea,' our mum said.

Ken rather doubted our mother's assertion regarding the players' allegiance to their families but said nothing on the subject.

'Well, Beryl, I'm sure this wonderful spread will cheer them up. It looks almost too good to eat.'

'I'm sorry tea's going to have to be so early, but we've got relatives coming up from London so I have to be there when they arrive,' Ivy explained.

'Don't fret, Ivy. I've told the umpire to take tea at three, in 15 minutes in fact. I'm sure young Roy will be able to hold the fort till then. In the meantime, I'll just try one of those ham and tomato ones, they look delicious.'

Ten minutes later Tom Buckle, the rather rotund wicketkeeper/batsman, was out, caught behind. Roy strode to the wicket and tried to persuade him to part with his pads. Given his shape and general lack of dexterity, removing pads was a sitting-down job for Tom. Roy, keen as mustard to get on with things, was virtually wrestling the pads from him.

Observing this debacle, the umpire looked at his watch. It was five to three.

'I think we'll call that tea, lads,' he said, and removed the bails.

When the fielding side arrived at the pavilion for an unexpected early tea they were overwhelmed by the spread our mum and Ivy had laid before them. They were, however, a little surprised that the home captain had ignored the convention of allowing the visitors to serve themselves first and was already tucking into the grub with gusto.

With tea over and his belly well and truly stuffed, Ken was ready to return to his normal position of No.4 batsman. However, he realised too late that Roy was already in the middle ready to face the next ball. On the one hand Ken was glad of the opportunity to let his tea go down, but more importantly wanted to get out there and continue to move the score along. His team had made an excellent start and Ken could see the prospect of reaching a good score by the end of the 40 overs. Nevertheless, his great asset as a captain was his calm, phlegmatic manner.

Ken leant back in his chair determined to enjoy the game. However, four overs later he was starting to get a bit on edge. Roy had largely kept the strike but had added only one run. He had watched Roy bat on a number of occasions and he could usually be relied upon to keep the score moving. Ken was only slightly concerned at this stage, but three overs later with Roy still hogging the strike without really scoring, he realised that something was going on. Somehow, the young man had got it into his head that he was there to protect his captain, although from what was not clear.

Drastic action was called for. After several unsuccessful attempts to get the attention of the other batsman, Tubby Pink, Ken sent the 12th man out to the middle on some spurious mission. His real purpose was to get a message to Tubby. As the 12th man returned to the pavilion Tubby looked over at his captain for confirmation. Like some Roman emperor of the past, Ken gave the sign to Tubby that his fellow gladiator should be sacrificed. The very next ball he called Roy through for a quick single and when Roy was almost upon him Tubby changed his mind and sent him back. Roy was run out at least four yards short of his ground.

'Hard luck, lad,' said Ken as he passed my disconsolate brother. 'I'll see if I can wrap things up from here.'

* * *

In professional cricket, as I'm sure Roy must have known, the nightwatchman is a lower-order batsman who comes in higher up the order than usual near the end of the day's play so as to protect other, more capable batsmen from being out cheaply. The idea is that he bats sensibly with a view to seeing out the day and still being there for the start of the following morning's play, hence the title 'nightwatchman'.

The use of a nightwatchman is something that goes in and out of favour in Test cricket rather like the use of the follow-on. Many captains continue to send in a nightwatchman to survive the last few overs left in the day. However, this tactic is disliked by some captains. Steve Waugh, for example, rarely used a nightwatchman during his captaincy of Australia, believing it to be a defensive tactic and he wanted his team to always be on the offensive. Similarly, Nasser Hussain described using a nightwatchman as a weakness.

In the modern game much is made of creating and maintaining a positive mindset and the concept of the nightwatchman runs contrary to this and risks handing back the initiative to the opposition. It does of course also mean that such players have to face the best bowlers. It is therefore not uncommon for the player to get out before the end of the day's play thus exposing the batsman, who he was supposed to be shielding, to batting in the twilight of the day anyway. Despite all this the notion of the nightwatchman remains and there is no obvious indication that this will change.

Their primary job is to stay at the wicket for long periods, keeping the strike wherever possible and holding one end up. In most circumstances there is no expectation on them to score many runs. For this reason the role is generally given to players who emphasise stout defence over quick run-scoring.

There is sometimes a need to be brave when the light is poor and the bowling hostile. Not all nightwatchmen rise to the challenge. On an infamous evening in 1976 when Brian Close and John Edrich were being battered by the West Indies pacemen at Old Trafford, the captain, Tony Greig, had to find someone prepared to pad up. Derek Underwood, at the time England's regular nightwatchman, refused point blank.

Generally speaking, it is a job for the taciturn, uncommunicative, undemonstrative guy, for the introverted, the obdurate. As suggested by Peter Carpenter's wonderful poem, it is a job for the man who least wants to be thrust into the limelight with a bat in his hand. Stand up, Jimmy Anderson, stoic and dogged, the man I instantly associate more than any other with this role.

Jimmy Anderson is England's longest-standing and most successful nightwatchman having survived into the next day on 26 of 28 occasions. On average he has faced more than 30 balls per innings in this role. However, Jimmy was not the perfect nightwatchman. On three occasions he unnecessarily exposed his partner and each time the batsman paid the ultimate penalty.

In 2008 against India he took a single that exposed Flintoff to the last three balls of the day. Flintoff was caught at short leg off the third.

Roy and I were present for the Ashes Test at Headingley in 2009 to see England go down to a crushing defeat by an innings and 80 runs. Near the end of the second day England had already lost four second innings wickets and defeat was probably already inevitable. Nevertheless, captain Andrew Strauss decided to deploy a nightwatchman. It was not Anderson's finest hour. Defying the conventions of how a nightwatchman should behave Anderson, who was on strike, called Alastair Cook for a leg bye off the first ball of an over. Cook was dismissed later in that same over and England ended the day on 82 for the loss of five wickets.

Worst of all was against Australia in Perth in 2010. Paul Collingwood, who had been under pressure following disappointing form with the bat, faced the last over of the day. He played the fifth ball behind square and called Jimmy through for an easy single. Anderson refused the run, leaving Collingwood to face the last ball of the day, which he edged to third slip and was caught.

The other England player I have seen many times dragging himself to the wicket at the end of the day's play is Matthew Hoggard. Hoggard took on the role on 14 occasions which is some feat given he professes to hate the job. In the following quote he also shows a degree of disdain for the top order batsmen who choose to deploy it: 'The one job that everyone quite blatantly tries to avoid is being nightwatchman, the bloke who has to come in to bat when nobody else wants to, a few overs before the close of play, when it's getting a bit dark and the precious, darling batsmen need to be protected.'

First and foremost, the job of a nightwatchman is to survive. In September 1955 at the Oval there was a player enlisted to this thankless task who appeared to do the exact opposite of what was required of him. In the end-of-season match between Surrey, the county champions, and The Rest Robin Marlar went in as nightwatchman for The Rest towards the end of the first day. He was stumped second ball for six! *The Times* observed that 'Marlar, the least watchful of watchmen one would have thought, was found wanting in his nocturnal duties.'

There have been cases where nightwatchmen have not only survived but have gone on to make significant scores. According to official statistics there are six occasions on which a nightwatchman has gone on to make a Test century, although two of these have been by the South African wicketkeeper/batsman, Mark Boucher. Roy and I have seen many splendid innings over the years from Boucher who often excels when his team are under the cosh. He is a genuine batsman with a Test average above 30. On the two occasions in question he came in at No.6 although listed as the No.7. I, along with many others, do not regard Mark Boucher as fitting the profile of a nightwatchman. There are therefore to my mind only four batsman in history who have managed this amazing feat.

Nasim-ul-Ghani of Pakistan became the first nightwatchman to score a century when he hit 101 against England at Lord's in 1962. He had made his debut in 1958, aged 16 years, and was at the time the world's youngest Test player.

In 1977 Tony Mann of Australia scored 105 as nightwatchman against India at Perth. In the fourth innings of the match the leg-spinner came out to bat at three as the nightwatchman and played out the day without a blemish. Australia still required 314 runs to win on the final day of the Test match. Instantly Tony went up a gear and hit ten boundaries in his century. Australia won the match by two wickets.

In 1979 Syed Kirmani, the Indian wicketkeeper, scored a hundred as a nightwatchman in Bombay against Australia. His innings of 101 not out lasted five hours.

However, none of these compared to the exploits of Jason 'Dizzy' Gillespie, the Australian pace bowler. In 2006, coming in to bat as nightwatchman on day two of the second Test against Bangladesh, he went on to make 201 not out. Albeit against a weak bowling attack, Gillespie's innings helped Australia win the game by an innings and 80 runs. Surely this is one record that will never be overtaken.

No English nightwatchman has ever scored a century although several have come close. In recent memory, Jack Leach scored 92 against Ireland at Lord's in 2019. After seeing off the final over of the day, Leach resumed the next morning and was only dismissed shortly before tea.

The best score from an English nightwatchman was achieved in 1999 by Alex Tudor, who scored an unbeaten 99 as he helped guide England to a seven-wicket win over New Zealand in Birmingham. Unfortunately for Tudor he got England over the line with a boundary, leaving himself just one short of his century.

* * *

It is undeniable that the deployment of a nightwatchman when wickets have fallen at the end of a day is, as Nasser Hussain believes, an act of weakness. Batsmen whose job it is to bat have decided along with their captain, who is almost certainly a batsman himself, that they may be unable to survive for a few late overs. So who has to go to face the music? A bowler, who might well have already sent down 20-plus overs that day and feel completely exhausted.

I have quoted Jimmy Anderson earlier and he does make a good case for cricket always being on the side of the batsman.

'If we were at war in ancient times we'd be the boulder carriers,'[3] he claims.

The use of a nightwatchman is above all a statement about the relative value of batsmen compared to bowlers.

'You've worked hard all day mate, but, guess what, it's your turn again.'

In international cricket a lot is made of the concept of 'team'. 'Team England, all for one and one for all.' But there is one man to whom this philosophy does not seem to apply. As the nightwatchman stands at the crease blinking into the fading light, his team-mates who make up the middle order sit with their feet up and as the final over begins the last of them bend down and with an air of relief start to unbuckle their pads. Nobody is watching him now as the conversation moves on to tomorrow and all the possibilities of doing well on a bright new morning. Perhaps it will be the day for that elusive hundred partnership. As he stands there resolutely, ready to face the opposition's best bowler, he knows beyond a shadow of doubt that he stands alone.

Chapter 23

Aspiring Young Cricketers

I HAVE covered in some detail my and Roy's cricketing exploits in which we displayed a lot of commitment and a modicum of talent. The little training we had came from our dad and one or two school teachers who put some time in because of their love of the game. Formal and consistent training was not available to young kids in those days, unless they were exceptionally talented and were linked to either a first-class county or a top public school. For working class youngsters like us any improvement in our skills with bat or ball came from persistence and from watching others.

Roy is a competent musician as well as a cricket lover but it is the former skill that he has handed on and nurtured with his children and grandchildren. His grandson Sam is already at age 13 a very talented guitarist. My eldest daughter, Emily, is also a musician, but that is nothing to do with her completely tone-deaf father.

What I have passed on to them is an all-consuming love of sport. At school Emily was captain of both the netball team and the hockey team and when she left her sister Lucy took over both roles. The two of them were also excellent athletes. Now as adults they have both recently taken up competitive sport again. Lucy's return to netball has unfortunately been interrupted by a serious ankle injury. Emily, who has always loved cricket, now plays for the women's team attached to Carmel, the same club where her son Finlay and daughter Iris play. Her husband Andy, to add some symmetry to the whole process, turns out for the same village team where I so ignominiously ended my playing days.

Both of Emily's children love their cricket and, unlike when I was a child, they each get formal training from a qualified coach every week. Iris is only ten but has shown herself to have some real ability as well as rather too much of her mum's competitive spirit.

Finlay, two years older, has already advanced to the next level and represents North Wales. Fin has genuine aspirations to make a living from cricket. Although we all know how hard that is, the whole family gives him the encouragement and support he needs.

Recently I went to watch Fin playing for North Wales. He bowled two tidy overs, taking one wicket. He then opened the batting. This started badly when he called for a run, resulting in the other opener being run out. It was not really Fin's fault as his opening partner was daydreaming rather than backing up. Fin got into a strop with himself as well as his team-mate and his mood did not really recover. Two overs later he was clean bowled for just one run. As he walked from the pitch steam was coming out of his ears, quite reminiscent of his mother when she found herself on the losing side whether playing hockey for the county or Ludo with her sister.

Fin needed some consoling on the day, but his response was to get home and practise the forward defensive for about two hours. In the next match he shared in a partnership of 87 with his captain, playing straight while his batting partner piled on the runs.

This episode led me to speculate on the traits that any aspiring sportsperson needs to succeed. Clearly one needs talent and good coaching, but tenacity, determination and focus also play a big part. Fin is obsessed with the game of cricket, playing, watching or practising at every opportunity. I can't remember the last time he came to see us without a bat in his hand.

In 2017 Roy and I arrived at our regular camping site, Thornton's Holt, on the Saturday lunchtime to watch a county match due to start the next day. We thought we would seek out some local cricket in the meantime. We did not have far to travel. Radcliffe-on-Trent Cricket Club play on a ground immediately adjacent to the campsite and so it was just a matter of finding a hole in the fence!

The game we watched was a second XI match from the South Nottinghamshire League and we were pleasantly surprised at the standard. Being familiar with club cricket I knew to expect the team to include one or two younger players and indeed Radcliffe's wicketkeeper did not seem any older than 15.

However, his junior status did not stop him carrying out an ongoing commentary on the match, nor did it deter him from dishing out advice to his senior team-mates. They all took it in good heart. He was not an exceptional keeper, but good to watch. His performance was a mixture of flamboyant takes, two superb catches and a number of miserable faux pas although he never seemed embarrassed by these. When it became Radcliffe's turn to bat he came out to open the innings and it soon became clear why he had been included. He was quite a small lad and not particularly powerful, but what he lacked in power he made up for in technique. He pulled off some lovely shots, not seeming at all fazed by the very quick opening bowlers. In fact the confidence he had shown as a wicketkeeper was also evident in his batting. The lack of boundaries meant that his progress was reasonably slow, but we could see that Radcliffe had uncovered a gem.

Roy and I were sitting near the pavilion and were both talking about him in glowing terms. Although the young man could easily be described as 'cocky' we were aware that a high level of self-confidence was a requirement for any aspiring sportsman. The guy sitting next to Roy was also showing a lot of interest in the young lad's performance.

Roy turned to talk to him. 'He's good, isn't he. Has he been playing with the adult team for long?'

'No, this is his first match for them. He only found out this morning that he was playing,' the chap replied.

'Well, he certainly looks confident,' said Roy. 'Have you seen him play before?'

'A few times, yes. I'm his dad.'

All three of us smiled.

'Well, you must be very proud of him,' said Roy.

His dad was obviously taking the whole thing very seriously. 'Let's see how he gets on first.'

We did not have long to wait. The very next ball he was given out lbw. He kicked the turf and headed for the pavilion. His dad rose to meet him as his role changed instantly from interested spectator to comforting parent. By the look on the lad's face his dad would have his work cut out.

So, is this hatred of losing displayed by Finlay and the young wicketkeeper/batsman positive or negative? Everyone who plays competitive sports likes to win and does not like to lose, but all of us at every level of sport experience both frequently. The critical issue is what happens next. Do we come to fear losing, allowing anxiety and doubts to grow, resulting in a gradual loss of confidence or do we bounce back, learning from the experience? We need to keep our focus on what we want to achieve in the next innings, consider what we could have done better last time and go out there and do it next time.

Finlay's immediate response to losing appeared negative, but he worked on what went wrong and performed better at the next opportunity. Also, the level of self-confidence displayed by the young lad playing for Radcliffe suggests he too can learn from losing.

Being honest with yourself regarding your own ability mixed with a determination to make the most of what talent you have is also an important trait. I can think of a number of players who were not exceptional but achieved levels of performance beyond what their talents suggested. A good example is Paul Collingwood. Never England's most gifted player, he demonstrated what could be achieved by tremendous fitness and application. Collingwood had a fine international career which included leading England to its first ever global tournament win, the 2010 World Twenty20. He was also a three-times Ashes winner. After retirement from international cricket, he continued to play for Durham until he was 42.

However, Collingwood had talent too and this remains the basic requirement.

In August 2017 Roy and I, now fully paid-up members of Nottinghamshire, decided we would spend a few days watching Notts' second XI. We had settled on the local derby between Notts and Derbyshire, a three-day game at the Barrow Turn ground at Swarkestone in Derbyshire.

Barrow Turn sits in the heart of the rural Derbyshire countryside. With pleasant views all round it is a very relaxed place to watch cricket.

The game turned out to be a fascinating choice. Second XI teams tend to be a mixture of young up-and-coming players and older players either coming back from injury or trying to find some form. For Notts a young Luke Wood stood out with bat and ball and a very young Lyndon James, aged only 18, scored 54 not out in the first innings and 40 in the second. James has now broken through into the Notts first team as an all-rounder but did not bowl at all in this match.

Most intriguing for us was a young bowler from Derbyshire. We had noticed the name Greg Cork on the team sheet and naturally wondered whether he was related to the great Derbyshire and England bowler, Dominic Cork. However, the moment he came on to bowl it was obvious that he was. We had a very clear memory of Dominic Cork's busy bowling style and in 1995 had witnessed his finest hour when he got a hat-trick against the West Indies at Old Trafford. His son's run-up and action were virtually identical to those of his father. Although he only took two wickets in the match he bowled 14 overs of which eight were maidens, again reminiscent of his dad. For a while afterwards I kept looking for his name on Derby's first XI team sheet, but he never quite made the grade and was released at the end of that season. He did play for a period in Australia, but I understand he now works for an IT solutions company. He had a lot going for him, but it seems he did not quite have the talent required.

I have no idea how Fin will fare. I am already realising it is harder to get recognised whilst living in North Wales as the chances of any county club noticing you are slim. My main hope is that cricket will always be a big part of his life and that he enjoys playing at whatever level he achieves. I think this much is already assured.

Chapter 24

Cricket Emerges from the Darkness into the Light

2019 HAD been billed as the greatest ever summer of cricket and it did not disappoint. In the World Cup during the closing stages of the round robin England did their best to throw it all away, but then recovered spectacularly to reach the final. It is now a matter of history that they won the incredible final 'by the barest of margins'. New Zealander Ian Smith, who had the unfortunate job of commentating on TV as his country lost the final for the second time in a row, rose superbly to the occasion.

'Two to win. Guptill's got to push for two. They've got to go. It's got ... the throw's got to go to the keeper's end ... He's got it! England have won the World Cup! By the barest of margins! By the barest of all margins!'

This amazing tournament was then followed by a highly competitive Ashes series, tied 2-2, that included Ben Stokes' Herculean effort at Leeds. It was in every way an incredible innings.

Roy and I extended our international season with a trip to Cape Town with the Barmy Army where we witnessed a fine and ultimately successful Test match against South Africa.

On the domestic front the contrast could not have been more pronounced. Roy and I made many pilgrimages to Trent Bridge during the 2019 season, always believing that the win would come. Were we being stoic or just kidding ourselves? The win never did come, and Nottinghamshire were relegated with ten defeats and four draws from their 14 games. Despite this we retained belief in the group of talented youngsters who we were sure would fire in 2020. By Christmas 2019 we had already renewed our membership.

We had tickets to watch England host Pakistan at Trent Bridge from 20–24 August 2020, in a match that was due to conclude the three-match series and bring down the curtain on the English Test summer. A joyful summer of cricket lay ahead.

And then everything changed. Soon after we arrived home from South Africa there were some stories about a nasty virus emanating from China, but it was a while until the full horror of Covid 19 unfolded.

The first impact on international cricket came with the indefinite postponement of the two-Test series against Sri Lanka that England had been set to play starting in Galle on 19 March 2020.

England were in the middle of a first-class warm-up match with a Sri Lanka Board President's XI when the announcement was made that the England squad and support staff would return to the UK.

While Roy and I had been with the Barmy Army at Cape Town we had made a number of friends and some of these were planning to tour Sri Lanka as well. As the news about the postponement was reported it was unclear to Roy and me whether these Barmy Army fans were already in Sri Lanka. Even if they were we felt sure they would deploy their humour and resilience to deal with whatever was thrown at them.

On 23 March the full lockdown began in the UK and from that point all organised sport was banned whether recreational or professional and that remained the case until the summer.

England was the first international side to grasp the nettle and invite the two teams they were due to meet, West Indies and Pakistan, to tour England despite the pandemic. To their great credit both teams agreed.

The two series were played in a bio-secure environment increasing organisational costs significantly on top of the loss of revenue through the absence of spectators. All matches were played at Old Trafford and the Rose Bowl in Southampton, both grounds having hotels on the premises.

The first Test against the West Indies took place in the aftermath of the death of George Floyd, killed by a white US police officer while his colleagues looked on. One of the highlights of the cricket summer was the impassioned statements made by West Indies legend Michael Holding and Ebony Rainford-Brent, the first black woman to play cricket for England, on Sky Sports on day one of the first Test. They called for the eradication of institutionalised racism for the good of humanity.

The cricket played during these two Test series was of the highest quality and the atmosphere between the players was friendly and respectful. For cricket-starved fans like Roy and me it was a lifeline that helped us both ease our way through the doom and gloom of life in a pandemic.

Given my desire to see as much cricket as possible I also tuned in for the T20 internationals. I have never been a great fan of this shortest form of the game. However, I have to say that the insight into the tactics of the game that I gained from listening to the Sky commentators, particularly Stuart Broad, helped me enjoy it a lot more.

County cricket took longer to get going, but when it did through the new Bob Willis Trophy it threw up some good matches. Unfortunately, this did not include any victories for Notts, although the young guns I referred to earlier did start to show some promise.

However, in the T20 format Notts did taste success. At Edgbaston on the first Sunday in October, Notts Outlaws memorably won the Vitality Blast for the second time in four seasons after easy victories over Lancashire and Surrey. The triumph was much deserved with Notts only losing one game out of 11.

Of course, no spectators were allowed to see any of the fixtures which had a disastrous effect on the finances of the club, in fact on professional cricket as a whole. Notts made a request to their members to consider leaving their membership fee in the club rather than seek a refund and both Roy and I agreed to do this.

Roy is a great fan of fifties comedian Tony Hancock and mimicked a scene from *The Blood Donor*.

'Do you think we'll get a badge? Nothing grand, a little enamel thing, a little motto that's all, nothing pretentious.'

In the event we got a county cap which was pretty cool.

For those like Finlay and Iris playing recreational cricket 2020 was very much an on-off season. It started badly on 23 June with Boris Johnson describing the cricket ball as 'a natural vector of disease', ruling out an imminent return of recreational cricket. However, shortly afterwards, in one of the government's more positive U-turns, it was given the go-ahead. During this period Fin did enough to find himself in the North Wales squad and in the summer of 2021 he got plenty of opportunities to play at this level.

In other sports the professional bodies also sought and found ways to enable events to take place with empty stadiums becoming an eerie reality in the UK and elsewhere.

There were exceptions, in particular in New Zealand, where the government's brilliant management of the pandemic allowed sport to continue relatively unaffected with spectators enjoying the live action. Under Prime Minister Jacinda Ardern, New Zealand took some of the swiftest and strongest actions against the outbreak and effectively eliminated Covid 19 in their country.

Although the pandemic had been badly mishandled during 2020, the spring of 2021 started to feel more optimistic as the effects of a highly efficient vaccine roll-out and a prolonged lockdown began to bear fruit.

In county cricket a new structure was devised to temporarily replace the existing first and second division and at last Notts started to live up to expectations.

In the new format the sides were separated into three initial seeded pools of six. Each side played the others in their pool home and away. The top two sides from each group then advanced to division one, with the others moving into divisions two and three. The winner of division one would be the county champions.

At the end of the first stage Notts were top of their group with four victories to their name, a big improvement on 2019 when they went the whole season without winning a match.

Roy and I were aware from the beginning of the season that there would be opportunities to watch some live cricket, albeit with limits on the numbers allowed. The first County Championship matches with socially distanced crowds were scheduled for 20 May including Notts hosting Worcestershire and we were determined to be there.

About ten days before this match, I thought I would go and watch a local game to put me in the groove of watching cricket again. In truth, I was so desperate to see some live cricket I would probably have watched Estonian ice cricket, if nothing else had been available. Carmel, the club where Fin and Iris play, did not have a first- or second-team fixture so I decided to go and watch a good village team about ten miles from home. Before I left Marieluise suggested I take one of our dogs, Cody, with me.

We had recently acquired two rescue dogs from Bulgaria, one of which was only eight months old. We had enlisted a dog trainer to help us teach Cody to come to his name and we were making some progress. As a security measure the dog trainer, Matt, had suggested we keep Cody on a long lead so that if he did not come at once we could give him a gentle tug to remind him. It also meant we would not lose him if things went wrong. We had been using one of the horse's lunge lines which was about 20ft long. Being with Cody at that time was fun, but not necessarily relaxing and I must admit I was not keen to take him to the cricket. However, Marieluise reminded me that he also needed to be socialised. I reluctantly agreed.

When I got to the enchanting old ground, surrounded by silver birch trees newly in leaf, I was relieved to see at least one other dog amongst the small crowd. The owner, a woman in her early sixties, soon made a beeline for us.

'What a cute little fellow,' she began and soon we were deep in conversation.

It turned out she was the wife of the club secretary and brought her little dog, rather similar to Tricky Woo of James Herriot fame, to every home game.

I was telling her about how we came to have dogs from Bulgaria when 'Tricky Woo', who was not on a lead, started running in circles around her. Soon Cody, with his long line trailing behind him, was in hot pursuit. I looked down with horror as I suddenly realised that Cody was roping her just as effectively as a cowboy might rope a steer. Before I could sound a warning Tricky Woo left the circle to run towards the pavilion and Cody tore after her. The ropes around the poor lady's legs suddenly tightened like a lasso with Cody bringing her to the ground like a well-trained vaquero. The poor woman squealed and tried to crawl towards Cody in order to release herself. Unfortunately, the sight of a grey-haired woman on her knees with desperation writ large across her face alarmed him and he took off again, pulling her knees from under her and flattening her on to her stomach.

Finally, I came to from the trance into which I had fallen and grabbed Cody before he could cause any more mayhem. Carefully I extricated the lady from the lariat and helped her to her feet. Not surprisingly she seemed to have changed her opinion of both me and Bulgarian rescue dogs. I tried to check her over, but she brushed me aside.

'Just go away and take that fiendish dog with you,' she shrieked.

I had to leave without seeing a single ball bowled.

On 20 May spectators, including Roy and I, returned to Trent Bridge for the first time in 608 days. Unfortunately the weather was awful, cold and damp, and we saw only 15 overs of cricket in a fragmented opening day. After several prolonged breaks for rain Nottinghamshire closed on 51/3. At the start of play there were more than 1,000 people looking forward to some cricket, but by the end we were amongst just a handful of intrepid supporters. This was not as we had envisaged our first match for nearly two years.

Roy and I were frozen the whole time, including at the campsite. We were reminded of the coldest ever Test match we had watched at Headingley in May 2007 when the temperature was 7.4°C. The weather conditions at Trent Bridge were similarly awful and the Worcestershire batsmen seemed to agree with us as they trudged on and off the pitch much as the West Indians had done 14 years earlier. More than half the match was rained off, but despite this Notts managed to forge a victory by an innings and 170 runs, dismissing Worcestershire for 80 and then 150 following on. Opening bowler Luke Fletcher was the star of the show, taking ten wickets in the match. This game came immediately after consecutive victories against Derbyshire and county champions Essex. Notts were set to have a much-improved season.

Our next opportunity to watch a County Championship match at Trent Bridge was in July against Derbyshire, which Nottinghamshire won by an innings and 36 runs inside three days. A notable event in this match was the unexpected debut of Dane Schadendorf, the second XI wicketkeeper/batsman. Regular first team wicketkeeper Tom Moores was injured and Ben Duckett was keeping in his place. By the end of day two he had reached 69 but failed to appear on day three, having been called up mid-game into the England ODI squad.

Instead Schadendorf appeared. He played really well showing no obvious nerves, scoring 24 in his only innings and taking four catches when Derbyshire batted again. Both Roy and I felt sympathy for Duckett who, following his dramatic call-up, failed to get a game.

Notts finished top of their group and so, with Warwickshire in second place, progressed to Division One. Counties carried forward half the points they scored from the two matches against the county in their original group and did not play that team in the divisional stage. Unfortunately, Notts' only defeats were in the two games against Warwickshire. As a result, they had the least points to carry forward and this turned out to be their undoing. In the end they finished third, just four points behind champions Warwickshire, despite emphatic victories at Trent Bridge against Lancashire, which Roy and I attended, and Yorkshire. It was an excellent season, despite the slightly disappointing outcome.

Roy and I had a long debate over whether to attend the first Test match at Trent Bridge against India from 4 August 2021. We had tickets for the first four days. On 19 July the government declared 'Freedom Day' in England, marking the end of social distancing and the compulsory wearing of masks at matches. The numbers of new Covid 19 infections were rising at an alarming rate and although we had both been 'double-jabbed' we did not feel immune. In the event, although we had tickets for the first four days we attended only the first two for which we had tickets in the pavilion. Given the heightened protocols to protect the players we felt relatively safe there.

It did not turn out to be the greatest of Test matches. On day one we experienced yet another England collapse, from 138/3 to 183 all out. Half of the second day was lost to rain. The game eventually ended in a draw.

At the time of writing the 2022 season is about to commence and despite a number of disappointments we are ready to go. As Notts fans we have had to cope with finding ourselves back in Division Two after the ECB announced that for 2022 the County Championship would revert to the two-division system with positions based on the 2019 league tables. Nevertheless, at every opportunity we will be there to cheer them on.

Like all England supporters we were traumatised by the Ashes debacle, but we have been there before. There are two exciting teams, New Zealand and South Africa, playing Test matches here this summer and those matches are to be relished. Our tickets are already organised.

Chapter 25

The Future for Cricket

IN THE summer period between the first two waves of Covid 19 Roy and I decided to try and replicate our normal experience of watching cricket together. Quite a lot of live cricket was being televised so we held regular video calls on Messenger during which we would watch the cricket, have a few pints together and generally chew the fat about our favourite sport.

First of all Roy had to subscribe to Sky Sports about which he was quite reluctant because of his antipathy to one man. He still remembered the Wapping dispute. Print unions tried to block distribution of the newspapers in Rupert Murdoch's News International group, after production was shifted to a new plant in Wapping in January 1986. At the new site, modern computer facilities allowed journalists to input copy directly, rather than involving print union workers. All of the workers were dismissed and the failure of the strike led to a general decline in trade union influence in the UK. For more than 30 years Roy had never bought any product controlled by Murdoch.

When I told Roy that Murdoch no longer had any stake in Sky he at first thought that I was telling fibs just to get him to subscribe. When I eventually persuaded him that it was true he took it as a personal victory and as justification for his 30-year boycott. Our dad had always told us to stick to our principles and I am sure he would have been proud of Roy's stand. Anyway, Dad hated Murdoch too!

I think Roy got some cut-price deal on the back of his daughter's TV subscription and as a result we had to start every video call by aligning our two televisions as Roy's broadcast was about 40 seconds behind mine. We first discovered this when I celebrated a West Indian wicket while on Roy's screen the bowler had not even started his run-up. After a few trial runs we eventually settled down to watch the matches together with a couple of pints lined up in front of us in case the tension got too much.

Watching international cricket in the strange silence of Test match grounds with no crowds took us on to a discussion about the future of our beloved game.

'On one level I don't know why we worry,' Roy began. 'There's no doubt that once this virus has passed we can go back to watching live cricket.' I nodded my agreement. 'What's more,' he continued, 'we'll be able to watch Test matches and county cricket for the rest of our lives. If things do change it won't happen that fast.'

We both fell silent and tried to block out any negative thoughts by concentrating on the live match being beamed into our living rooms by Sky. England were attempting to win the third Test against the West Indies and take the series. It was looking odds-on that they would succeed.

What Roy had said was true, but we both knew that we cared deeply about the future of cricket. Pretending that we were only worried about what would or wouldn't happen in the next 15 years; well, we were just kidding ourselves.

Roy made another stab at optimism. 'As long as I can remember people have been predicting the demise of cricket, particularly the longer form of the game, but so far it hasn't happened. I think maybe we worry too much.'

I looked at him long and hard. 'Maybe.'

At that moment on our TV screens Stuart Broad had Kemar Roach caught in the slips for a duck. The West Indies were nine down for just 188 runs and Stuart had five wickets for the umpteenth time in his international career. He had also batted at No.10 and scored 62 off just 45 balls.

'To think the stupid bastards dropped him for the first Test and here he goes again with a man of the match performance.'

'Stupid bastards,' Roy muttered in confirmation.

If there was one thing we could agree on it was our outrage that England had left our favourite Nottinghamshire player out of the first Test. In typical fashion he had come bouncing back with six wickets in the next match and here he was again cutting through the West Indies batting line-up like a knife through butter.

'I don't think they'll be dropping him again in a hurry,' Roy predicted, no doubt accurately.

Before we had a chance to savour the moment the adverts came on, putting us back into reflective mode.

'Do you think we'll ever take in another tour?' I asked him.

'I can't see why not, once our funds have recovered from the South Africa trip. Where would you fancy?'

I had expected this question and I had a ready answer. 'I'd love to watch us play West Indies in Antigua.'

Roy had always been a big fan of West Indian cricket and many of their famous fast bowlers ranked high in his estimation. In recent years they had become a much-diminished force in world cricket and he had no desire to see them thrashed, even by England. However, the signs were there that they were again on the up and had proved as much a few weeks earlier by winning the first Test.

'If we were to do that I just hope that the crowds recover,' he said. 'They've been playing home matches to empty stadiums for some time now. If we went with the Barmy Army we'd probably outnumber the home crowd.'

I was aware of this possibility, but to be honest my choice was as much to do with the beauty of the island as it was with the cricket. I was pretty sure what Roy's choice would be, but I asked him anyway.

'I'd love to do Australia again, maybe Sydney. Surely it's not impossible to win over there and for us to see it.'

It wasn't impossible, but let's just say I had done the maths!

The adverts were over and we turned our attention back to the current game. England only needed one more wicket to wrap up the West Indies' first innings. We didn't have long to wait. In his next over Broad bagged the wicket of Shane Dowrich, the West Indian wicketkeeper who had been showing some resistance. The West Indies were all out for just 197 and Stuart Broad had six wickets. Cue adverts!

Gently, almost reluctantly, we returned to our discussion about the future of cricket.

'Think back to when we were kids,' I suggested. 'In summer most of us played some cricket, even if they were just scratch games with four or five on each team.'

Roy nodded. 'Remember the blokes we toured Australia with in 2006? Most of them were between 50 and 60. Every one of them had played cricket at some level.'

'I know. If cricket is to remain popular in this or any other country then people need to play the bloody game.' I paused for a moment as my thoughts moved to the spectators at Trent Bridge. 'Even in the summer holidays not that many youngsters come to watch the county matches. And those that do, well you can tell by listening to them chatting. They all play cricket.'

We had both remarked on this several times when we found ourselves seated close to groups of young lads or a couple of youngsters watching with their dad.

'The thing is, Geoff, it's a complicated game. If you don't play the game you're not going to enjoy watching it. I mean any stupid bastard can understand football, even if they'd just arrived from Mars.'

Overall participation rates for cricket in this country are already low and getting lower. In 2016 158,500 adults played cricket in England once a week, less than one-tenth of the number who played football and down by almost 37,000 from a decade before. This is quite an alarming drop.

'The trouble is,' I ventured, 'they just don't play cricket in state schools anymore.'

When we were young Roy went to the local high school which had cricket teams for every school year as well as a first team largely made up from the sixth form, but also including younger lads with particular talent. Consequently, Roy played representative cricket throughout his school life.

I continued with my theme. 'Finlay is soon to start at one of the best high schools in the area. It's a school with a sport and leisure centre attached which is available to the school during school hours throughout term time which is brilliant. The school has a fantastic sporting reputation ...'

'You're not going to tell me they don't play cricket!'

'His dad rang the school a few weeks back and they don't have any organised cricket teams. I couldn't believe it.'

'Is he still playing for your local club? I'm sorry I've forgotten what it's called,' Roy asked.

'Carmel. Yes he is, thank God. I had hoped that playing for the school would sort of take over. Me and his mum and dad spend hours each week taking him to cricket matches and practice as well as his sister. Looks like we're going to have to carry on.'

Just at that moment the England openers came out to start their team's second innings. There were just four overs due before the lunch break, always a tricky time.

'I really hope Burns and Sibley can establish themselves as England openers. They make a bloody good combination; Burns pushes the score along and Sibley is a proper old-fashioned opener.'

'Boring, you mean.'

'I can do boring,' Roy stated firmly. 'That innings we saw in Cape Town was perfect. He batted slowly, but never looked like getting out. Just what the doctor ordered. It means the strokemakers can come in after him without the anxiety of a potential collapse.'

As hoped, Roy's favoured opening pair saw off the four overs without incident. The umpires removed the bails to indicate it was time for lunch.

'What a civilised game!' Roy declared as he prepared to go off air to attend to his own lunch. 'I assume Marieluise has already done yours!' Those were his final words before the screen abruptly went blank.

Roy and I had left it open whether we got together on Messenger for the afternoon and evening sessions. In the event we both had things to do and so decided against it. It may seem strange that we were less interested because England were so dominant thus taking a lot of the tension out of the match. Most sports fans will understand this. Both of us got on with our chores with the TV on in the background. England were going like a steam train and reached 226/4 in just 58 overs. I think the captain, Joe Root, was giving his partner Burns the opportunity to reach a hundred, but when he was out for 90 Root declared the innings and put the West Indies in to bat. Enter stage left

Stuart Broad, who claimed two wickets in his three overs. These were his 498th and 499th Test wickets in his career and I found myself fumbling for my tablet to contact Roy so we would see his 500th together. However, before I could get through the umpires decided it was the close of the day's play. Broad was left to envisage what his 500th wicket might look like, but like us would have to wait for the event itself.

When I got up the next morning it was pouring down and continued to rain for hours. Manchester, where the game was being played, is only 60 miles from us and has the worst reputation for rain anywhere in the country. It was not necessary to consult BBC weather to see if it was raining there too. As it turned out the game was completely washed out on that day, but England still had a day left to wrap up the game and the series.

Having the bit between my teeth regarding the potential demise of cricket I decided to spend some of the day on the internet checking some things out. Of particular interest to me was the effect on audiences from live cricket moving behind a paywall.

I am a great admirer of the quality of the cricketing product provided by Sky, even though I too have no time for Rupert Murdoch. I am also aware that the relationship between Sky and the England and Wales Cricket Board (ECB) brings a lot of revenue into the game, some of which, I am told, feeds down into junior cricket, although I have not seen that much evidence of it. However, since 2005, the last time a Test match was shown live on 'free to air' television, I was sure there had been a significant reduction in the size of the cricket audience. How right I was. I could barely believe the figures I uncovered and was eager to share the results of my research with Roy.

The following morning we joined up on Messenger five minutes before the start of play, eager to be 'together' when

Broad got his 500th wicket. We did not have long to wait. After just five overs there was a short break for rain and almost immediately after the players came out again Broad trapped Kraigg Brathwaite lbw. Only one other England bowler, Jimmy Anderson, had reached this milestone and ironically poor Brathwaite was Anderson's 500th victim too. It was a shame for Broad that he achieved this at an empty stadium, but if the smile on his face was anything to go by he did not seem to mind.

After all the excitement and copious replays of Broad's most famous wickets Roy and I settled back to watch the rest of the match. After my research the day before I was keen to restart the discussion about the future for cricket.

'There's always a lot of speculation about the effect of terrestrial television losing live cricket, so I …'

'Speculation, my arse,' Roy interrupted. 'It's bloody obvious that moving live cricket to Sky is killing the game.'

'Well, it looks like you could be right,' I replied. 'I had a look on the internet yesterday to compare the viewing figures.'

'Well, go on then.'

'Obviously the most popular spectacle is the Ashes so I compared 2019 with 2005, which was the last time a Test match was live on Channel 4. Not surprisingly, Ben Stokes' Ashes heroics at Headingley saw Sky record its highest ever audience for one day of live Test cricket. A peak of 2.1 million UK viewers switched on to see the finish. That is miles above their normal viewing figures which are usually well below a million. In fact, in the 2015 Ashes viewing figures rarely went above half a million.'

'Yeh, well that was a pretty special innings from Stokes, but I bet even more watched in 2005.'

'To try and make a valid comparison I looked at the figures for the climax of the Trent Bridge Test in 2005.'

This was the unbelievably tense match we attended with Emily and Andy when Shane Warne almost, but not quite, robbed us of a certain victory. Roy had a DVD of the match and had often told me that when he watches it he still worries that we might not win!

'So let's have it,' he demanded.

'8.4 million watched the climax,' I announced. 'That was more than half of the total of people watching any TV anywhere in Britain.'

Roy looked smug. 'QED!'

Roy and I were just getting back to watching the current game when Finlay appeared at the living room window. Emily and Andy keep their caravan at our place and Andy had come over to practise erecting his new awning. Fin had accompanied him ostensibly to help, but when Marieluise told him Roy was in town, albeit virtually, he left his dad to it and came straight over. Emily and Andy continue to be part of our group when Roy and I get tickets for live international cricket and for the last few years Finlay and Iris have been included as well. Consequently, Roy and Fin have met several times at matches. Fin loves sitting next to Roy who is so knowledgeable about the game and its history and Fin just sits and soaks it all up. With all the stuff he reads about the modern game plus what he learns from Roy he is well on the way to becoming a human cricket encyclopaedia.

Throughout the whole Covid experience during 2020 Marieluise and I refrained from joining any 'bubble' and that meant we were still socially distancing from our daughters and their families. Fin needed no reminding of what this meant and in no time at all he had opened the living room window wide and was sitting outside, framed in the window, on top of one of my stepladders. From there he could watch the match on my TV and join in our conversation.

Soon Roy was asking him about his club, Carmel.

'We're supposed to be allowed to play again now, but we haven't yet,' Fin told him. 'I think our coach Alun is still a bit nervous about it.'

'Your dad said they might start with a few games between the Carmel players,' I reminded him.

'I don't care. Any game is fine. I just wanna play.'

'I'm sure it won't be long,' Roy reassured him.

At that moment Chris Woakes, England's third seam bowler, got the wicket of Shai Hope, inevitably caught by Stuart Broad.

When the adverts came on I told Fin what we had been discussing although I tried to put a more hopeful gloss on the subject. To Fin cricket is everything and any suggestion that it could be on the decline would hit him badly. Like all kids in 2020 he had already had far too much to worry about without me adding to the burden.

In no time the three of us were discussing the role of small clubs like Carmel in keeping interest in cricket alive. Cricket is expensive. You need a proper pitch, proper gear to play it and people and children who want to give time to it. There is a lot of competition for young people's attention from the web, gaming, mobile technology and social media and of course from other sports. It is here that many small clubs across England and Wales play such a vital role. Those like Carmel that have junior sections are always on the lookout for youngsters to take part. However, despite their best efforts, many of these clubs struggle to maintain junior teams through lack of numbers, forcing them to field teams of mixed ages or go a whole season without junior representation.

Given that Fin had been playing junior cricket for quite a few years and I had been watching him and his sister, we were able to tell Roy about all the efforts that clubs make to give kids a good experience. Junior cricket is organised in a way that keeps children involved in a game throughout with rules to ensure nobody goes for long periods without batting or bowling. Also the training is based around having fun while learning the skills.

As well as the efforts made by the clubs there are initiatives like the All Stars Cricket programme that try to get boys and girls aged 5–8 into the game. The problem is how to get children and young people to seek out opportunities to play cricket in the first place. Most of the young people that play alongside Finlay and Iris have ended up playing cricket because they have a parent or grandparent who loves the game. It is not common for children whose family have no attachment to cricket to spontaneously become interested in the sport.

With football it is entirely different. Firstly, all that is needed for a group of kids to enjoy a game is a football and a few jumpers as goal posts. Secondly, football can be seen everywhere including on terrestrial television. Children have every opportunity to watch their heroes on TV and soon form allegiances to teams and inevitably want to play themselves.

Fin then told us about something he had done at school which confirmed much of what we had been talking about.

'I took a picture of Joe Root [England's cricket captain] into school a few weeks ago and showed it to all my mates in the class. Only one of 'em, Leanne, could say who it was! How could you not know who Joe Root is?'

At this point Andy joined Fin at the window and after saying hello to Roy and checking the score of the match he dragged a very reluctant young cricketer off to help him with his confounded awning.

In terms of the number of people who follow it, cricket is widely seen as the world's second most popular sport,

CRICKET, MY BROTHER AND ME

with football obviously taking the number one spot. However, to a large extent this results from its popularity in India with a population of 1.3 billion. In reality cricket, whilst statistically popular, has not significantly increased its following outside of the United Kingdom and those countries that were previously part of the British Empire.

In contrast football is perhaps the only sport which can really be regarded as a global game, as demonstrated by the viewing figures at each World Cup. Within any given country, most people will be able to explain how the game is played, and the majority of them will watch it from time to time. Most countries on the other hand have only the vaguest understanding of how cricket is played.

Even in cricketing strongholds there are problems, the most serious being the apparent fall in popularity amongst young people. Throughout the 1970s and 1980s the West Indies team dominated world cricket and is now widely regarded as having been one of the best in Test cricket's history. During this period cricket's position as the No.1 sport in the Caribbean was undisputed. Now more young people play football and basketball than cricket. As a result the West Indies cricket team has declined significantly and there are plenty of empty stadiums there when cricket is played, even for international Test matches.

South Africa continue to have a strong cricket team with significant black representation, but it is not the favourite sport for either the white or the black population. The best-loved sport in the black community is football and in the white community rugby is clearly the most popular.

The vast majority of professional cricketers in South Africa are educated in the private sector and that is even true for some of the new black stars like Kagiso Rabada, Lungi Ngidi and Andile Phehlukwayo. So, the increased involvement of black youngsters in organised sport is not likely to significantly alter the popularity of cricket. Attendance at Test matches is also a concern. Roy and I visited Cape Town for the New Year Test in 2020 where the legions of England supporters easily outnumbered the home crowd.

Even in New Zealand the crowds at cricket matches, particularly for the long game, have been in decline for some time. It is now only in England, Australia and India where international cricket draws huge crowds.

In 2009 a terrorist attack on the Sri Lankan team bus outside the Gaddafi Stadium in Lahore forced the suspension of international cricket in Pakistan. It had a massive effect on an otherwise flourishing game that has a huge following in the country. Pakistan went more than a decade without hosting a home Test match, having to play their 'home' games in the United Arab Emirates.

There have been a few limited-over tours to Pakistan in the last four years and top-flight cricketers are slowly trickling back in, primarily playing in the Pakistan Super League, but there is still some way to go before international cricket is properly reinstated.

Pakistan received plaudits from across cricket for their decision to tour England in 2020, in the midst of the coronavirus pandemic. This series was due to take place soon after the conclusion of the West Indies series which we were currently watching. As a result a number of significant people involved in English cricket, not least the Test captain Joe Root, have acknowledged that they owe Pakistan cricket a huge debt. What better way would there be to repay that debt than through an England tour?

The signs in the country indicate that the popularity of cricket in Pakistan remains high and it is to be hoped that when things return to normal the crowds will come flooding back.

All the issues that we discussed have impacted on the popularity of cricket. Few state schools have cricket teams; it can rarely be seen on free to view TV; fewer people are playing cricket and fewer people are watching it. The authorities are naturally concerned and a number of strategies are in motion to revive its popularity in cricket countries and spread the game beyond the already established cricket nations.

But how do you make a deeply complicated game, with quirky rules and idiosyncratic vocabulary, that is often derided as boring, palatable to a new audience? Given this difficulty, the main strategy has been the development of a shorter and more understandable form of the game: T20 cricket.

T20 cricket has been developed to try and win new audiences for the sport. With this the cricketing authorities have achieved considerable success. Ironically Roy and I worry that the strategy to ensure cricket's survival could be the very thing that sees off that form of the game that the purists like us most relish.

For now we were happy just to watch the Test match currently on offer, England versus West Indies. In the end the game came to a satisfying conclusion: England won by 269 runs, as a result also winning the series, and Stuart Broad was named man of the match.

During our chats about the possible demise of our favourite game it was Roy who more often hit a pessimistic note, so as the West Indies series came to a close I asked him the ultimate question.

'So is cricket doomed in the long term?'

'Doomed? Don't be daft! People have been playing it since the early 16th century, so why stop now? We're handing the baton on to the likes of Iris and Finlay and this process is repeated all over the civilised world. And don't worry, when they're old and stupid like us they'll be handing it on again.'

Postscript

SPORT HAS been good to me, and although it has occasionally sent me into the doldrums it has massively enhanced my life and I thank my dad for making me a sports fan, some might say a sports fanatic. In time, with luck, it is only the great days that really stick in your mind.

I have had my own personal highs. Winning the high jump at the school sports day was a great feeling with the added boost of discovering I had set a new school record. Topping that was the pride I felt 25 years later when I returned to my old school to watch a sports day only to find my name in the programme still as the long jump record holder.

I have turned out to play for my village football team in the Umbro Vets Cup to face the stars of Everton's glorious past where I had the dubious pleasure of marking Northern Irish international, Bryan Hamilton.

And I have been there with my brother on cherished occasions like Stuart Broad's 8-15 in the Ashes at Trent Bridge and to see Kevin Pietersen demolish the great South African bowling attack at Headingley.

Some moments I have experienced through TV and radio, often with passionate commentary to enhance the action. England winning the Rugby World Cup and recently the Cricket World Cup were massive moments although I was not there to see them live.

In 1966 I was 15 and Roy was 17. He had just been on holiday to Spain with a group of friends and was due back on the day of the World Cup Final. In those days it was common to travel by ferry and Roy was due to arrive back mid-morning in Southampton. My dad and I drove down to pick him up knowing we had more than enough time to get home and watch the final. Unfortunately, the ferry was more than three hours late.

By the time we had found Roy it was less than an hour to kick-off. We had no hope of getting home in time. My dad had a sudden brainwave. Although it was far from ideal we decided to go into town and find a TV shop. In those days there were plenty of small shops that sold or rented televisions and they always had a selection of their products, switched on, in the window. In no time at all we had found a Radio Rentals, who at the time had about 500 shops. It was strange watching with no sound, but at least we could see it.

We thought we were home and dry after Martin Peters put us ahead with just 12 minutes left, but in the last minute Wolfgang Weber equalised, sending the game into extra time. We were devastated and also pretty weary, but we remained stoic, ready to face another half hour of play. Just as the game was about to restart the shop manager came out and ushered us inside. He put four chairs out and sat down beside us to watch the final 30 minutes. We were mightily grateful. The added bonus was that we could now hear the electrifying commentary by the BBC's Kenneth Wolstenholme including the famous line as England scored their fourth in the last moment of the match: 'And here comes Hurst. He's got ... some people are on the pitch, they think it's all over. It is now!'

My favourite radio memory of all was stopping suddenly in a lay-by on the way home from our holiday in Devon in 1991. I feared, if I did not stop, I would crash the car. It was the final event of the Tokyo World Athletics Championships, the men's 4×400 relay. Roger Black was running the first leg and my then 12-year-old daughter, Emily, was screaming, 'C'mon Roger, c'mon Roger' in my ear. I did an emergency stop into the lay-by and Emily, Lucy and I jumped out of the car and flung all the doors open to maximise the volume from the crackly radio. I think my wife thought there was a genuine emergency. For Emily, her sister Lucy and me there was.

In the end it came down to the final leg, with Kriss Akabusi, a hurdler, on the shoulder of the American Antonio Pettigrew, individual 400m gold medallist. Surely the gold medallist would easily beat off the challenge, but as they entered the home straight Akabusi strained every sinew as did the commentator. As the passing drivers stared at us and gave us a wide berth we roared him home. Sport at its most glorious.

References

1: Flintoff, Andrew, *Being Freddie* (Hodder & Stoughton, 2005)

2: Warne, Shane, *No Spin* (Ebury Press, 2018)

3: Anderson, Jimmy, *Bowl. Sleep. Repeat.* (Cassell, Octopus Publishing Group, 2019)

4: Stokes, Ben, *On Fire* (Headline Publishing Group, 2019)

5: Henderson, Michael, *That Will Be England Gone* (Constable, 2020)

6: Liew, Jonathan, *LBW was conceived in a different era of cricket's history – it's time to modernise this outdated law* (The Independent Newspaper, 2017)

7: Jessop, Gilbert, *Cricket* (London: C Arthur Pearson, 1903)

8: Wilde, Simon, *Wisden Cricketers of the Year: A Celebration of Cricket's Greatest* (Wisden, 2013)

9. Peter Carpenter, *After the Goldrush* (Nine Arches Press, 2009)